RYAN ENNISS is a playwright, actor and voice-over artist originally from Tasmania, currently based in Sydney. Ryan holds a Bachelor of Contemporary Arts (Theatre) from the University of Tasmania, as well as a Bachelor of Fine Arts (Acting) from the National Institute of Dramatic Art (NIDA).

Drizzle Boy won the 2022 – 2023 Queensland Premier's Drama Award, and was the first mainstage show in Australian history to feature an autistic lead, as well as be written by an autistic playwright.

His published works include the award-winning *Watching*, as well as other plays such as *(Dis)cord*, *Data Management* and *The 2100 Club*. In his sparse specks of spare time, Ryan enjoys listening to heavy metal, going for walks in nature, and drinking more tea than his dentist would like him to.

Daniel R. Nixon, Kevin Spink and Naomi Price in Queensland Theatre's DRIZZLE BOY, *2023 (Photo: Brett Boardman)*

Drizzle Boy

RYAN ENNISS

CURRENCY PRESS
The performing arts publisher

CURRENCY PLAYS

First published in 2024
by Currency Press
Gadigal Land, Suite 310, 46-56 Kippax Street, Surry Hills NSW 2010, Australia
enquiries@currency.com.au
www.currency.com.au

Typeset by Brighton Gray for Currency Press.
Cover design by Rochelle Oh for Currency Press.

Currency Press acknowledges the Traditional Owners of the Country on which we live and work. We pay our respects to all Aboriginal and Torres Strait Islander Elders, past and present.

A catalogue record for this book is available from the National Library of Australia

Contents

Daniel R. Nixon in Queensland Theatre's Drizzle Boy, *2023 (Photo: Brett Boardman)*

Drizzle Boy was first produced by Queensland Theatre at the Bille Browne Theatre, Brisbane, on the lands of the Jagera and Turrbal people, on the 16 March 2023, with the following cast:

DRIZZLE BOY	Daniel R. Nixon
MOTHER / JULIET / VALENTINA TERESHKOVA / DUSTIN HOFFMAN / SPEAKER / DOCTOR	Naomi Price
FATHER / HANS ASBERGER / BAPHOMET / SPEAKER / DOCTOR / DUSTIN HOFFMAN / SPEAKER / DOCTOR	Kevin Spink

Director, Daniel Evans
Set and Costume Designer, Christina Smith
Lighting Designer, Matt Scott
Composer/Sound Designer, Guy Webster
Video Designer, Nevin Howell

Drizzle Boy was the winner of the Queensland Premier's Drama Award 2022–23 and presented with the support of Griffith University and the Queensland Government.

Daniel R. Nixon and Naomi Price in Queensland Theatre's DRIZZLE BOY, 2023 (Photo: Brett Boardman)

Introduction

'The beauty of a living thing is not the atoms that go into it, but the way those atoms are put together.'
—Carl Sagan

A play is a living thing—it fights for breath, flexes its muscles, learns to crawl, stand (often only to fall over in the second act) and then begins to find its voice, to speak to us. All the while, the playwright wills it into being—coaxing, cutting, creating—making it stronger, more supple, more exact until that amorphous draft (Draft 10 … Draft 12.4 … FinalDraft_03 … FinalFINALDraft_10) concentrates and crystallises into something unexpected, a little cosmic and really *really* beautiful.

You are holding such a thing.

I first encountered Ryan Enniss' play in the Queensland Premier's Drama Award. I hadn't read the script or seen the first public reading but it had made an impression on a number of people who were there and even then—in its infancy—there was genuine excitement: 'there's a scene where the parents drink bleach and die!' … 'that bit where he goes to space?' … 'and who is that Baphomet guy?!'

When I first read the play (and shortly thereafter met Ryan) I remember being struck that his play was him … or maybe an extension of him. Ryan is a person of daring imagination and acidic wit. He also writes quicker than any other playwright I've met and this speed is matched only by his deft ability to slip in and out of characters' voices right in front of you.

Ryan's frame of reference ranges from the fantasy of *Adventure Time* through to the magic of *Dungeons & Dragons*, and because of this, the work is energetic and fantastical—playing fast and loose with historical figures and Franken-doctors while raging along to the rhythm of Ryan's favourite genre of music: heavy metal. And yet, though the work is sometimes frenetic, often tongue-in-cheek and, okay, a little profane: he and his play possess a real sense of tenderness.

Scenes are indexed with real galactic coordinates. There are moments of ghostly suburban quiet. Bouquets of frangipanis. Great swirls of synaesthesia sound and colour. The relentless pursuit of deep-space silence. And lots and lots of stars. These moments are my personal favourite—they shimmer amongst the mounting anarchy as Drizzle Boy loses control of his finely-tuned world. These quiet moments light the way towards that ending (... you'll see). I think they're born from a writer who is deeply interested in nature—both human and environmental. Consistent maybe with an artist who describes himself as 'the shyest person ever' who grew up on a property in Tasmania where he 'could scream into the wild blue yonder and no-one would hear you.' When he moved to Sydney to study acting, that 'yonder' looked a little different: 'I miss going out and seeing the stars rather than the light pollution.'

Drizzle Boy is the story of an autistic young man who is beginning undergraduate university study in the hopes of one day becoming an astronaut. In the opening scene, Drizzle Boy says to his new friend Juliet:

> DRIZZLE BOY: Once I've finished this course I want to get a masters degree, which I'll use to get a job for my two years' relevant work experience with either NASA or JAXA, which is the Japanese Aerospace Exploration Agency. Then it's a simple matter of learning Japanese, passing the physical exam, completing ten months of intensive training, and surviving the rocket launch. Oh, and I'm autistic.

All fairly straightforward ... until he begins to realise that the power structures around him are conspiring to place the stars firmly out of his reach.

> DRIZZLE BOY: [*To the audience*] [...] I feel ... bad. I feel angry. So angry. And it's no-one's fault, my fault, your fault, just because someone sitting in a skyscraper somewhere decided that I shouldn't move my hands too much, or look away from someone when they're talking, or think in colours. The world was built not welcoming of anyone but those who built it, and when others struggle to live in it, the builders have the audacity to tell those struggling that they should never have been born in the first place.

Ryan has said that this is a story about his coming of age—and it is—but what I came to realise in staging this play is that it is also a coming-of-age story for many of *us*. It's about recognising the way in which we might be complicit in preventing someone from reaching their full potential, and how everyone—no matter how they think or interpret the world—should ever have to dream smaller for the sake of fitting in.

Drizzle Boy is a write-back, a clarion call and an anthem for anyone who's ever felt a little lost, out of step, with the world around them. It honours the enormous courage it can sometimes take to carve out your own corner of the galaxy—to fight for its place, to protect it from those who'd take it away, to open it out to others and say: 'this is me, this is where I am, right here is where I belong.'

'Drizzle Boy should never leave the stage,' Ryan writes in the preface to the play, 'because as everyone knows, autistic people are the centre of the universe and everything revolves around them.' Despite many drafts, this foreword has never changed. And, quite appropriately, this became the portal into the debut production for the entire creative team. When we worked to bring Drizzle Boy's universe to life—we always wanted to ensure that it was the audience who were entering Drizzle Boy's space … and not the other way round.

To this end, designer Christina Smith conceived an orbiting world unto itself—a deep blue mirrored disc that is an homage to space craft, planetariums and the concentric circular maps of Copernicus. The design behaved almost like a blueprint for Drizzle Boy's internal imaginative space where time is temporal, flashbacks land like lightning bolts, painful memories bubble to the surface and sideways fantasies spontaneously erupt into life.

It was an honour to work alongside both Ryan and actor Daniel R. Nixon (who originated the title role), and to have met a constellation of many excellent advocates and allies of autism. Daniel and Ryan both found theatre because they love to tell stories but, more importantly, right now, they need to tell their stories their way.

It's DB who borrows the maxim: 'If you've met one autistic person, you've met one autistic person' and, from the outset, Ryan has always openly acknowledged that Drizzle Boy is only a beginning:

Strangely enough, the experience of a young, white, verbal man is the most commonly presented version of autism within media. And yet, I have still somehow never seen an authentic representation of myself on stage or screen. No, autistic people are relegated to the side characters, often for comedic, or tragic effect, and often their 'condition' is cause for much concern. But that doesn't represent me. Nor anyone else I know that is autistic. I only wish that there was space for even more diverse stories to be included in this script, but alas, there are only so many minutes in a play. For women, BIPOC, and LGBTQIA+ autistic people, know that you are not alone. I see you, and hope that Drizzle Boy inspires, empowers, and makes space for you, and your stories.*

There is 'all kinds of magic', a whole load of atoms swirling about in these pages—amongst them space bears, high-school formals, one or two broken hearts, rocket launches, Russian cosmonauts and Dustin Hoffman—but standing back and looking at Ryan's play: the beauty is in how they have all been put together in this living thing.

My hope is that Drizzle Boy finds his way onto many stages, into many rocket launches, starry vistas and the hearts and heads of people who need to hear him … until, eventually, self-determined stories like Ryan Enniss' *Drizzle Boy are* no longer the exception, they're the rule.

Daniel Evans

---

* Playwright's Note, *Drizzle Boy* program

Daniel R. Nixon and Kevin Spink in Queensland Theatre's Drizzle Boy, *2023 (Photo: Brett Boardman)*

CHARACTERS

DRIZZLE BOY

BAPHOMET

STUDENT, voiceovers—there are three, and should be voiced by multiple actors

JULIET

HANS ASPERGER

MOTHER

FATHER

ATTENBOROUGH, voiceover

VALENTINA TERESHKOVA

SPEAKER

DOCTOR, voiceovers—there are several, and can be played by multiple actors

LOTTO ANNOUNCER, voiceover

DUSTIN HOFFMAN

MUSEUM WORKER, voiceover

SOLAR TOUR GUIDE, voiceover

AUTISM TALKS, voiceover

BILL THE SPACE BEAR

YOUNG WOMAN

NOTES

The setting is Drizzle Boy's psychological and/or imaginative space.

Drizzle Boy must be played by a neurodivergent actor. Drizzle Boy should never leave the stage, because as everyone knows, autistic people are the centre of the universe and everything revolves around them.

INFINITY

The heavens roll over everything, billions of points of light bathe the space in a soft glow. Enter DRIZZLE BOY, *who is in a state of unreadiness. There is a small soft toy bear, wearing a space suit: Space Bear.*

DRIZZLE BOY: [*to the audience*] Hello. Hello, everyone, are you all comfortable? Strapped in? Good. I'd like to take the opportunity now, to tell you about the wonders of my universe. The universe in which I am at the centre. [*To Space Bear*] Too much?

> DRIZZLE BOY *puts on his socks, pants and shoes.*

[*To the audience*] Seeing as this is my universe, I feel I should let you in on a few rules. Rule number one: I am going to talk to you sometimes, so prepare for that. Today is my first day of university. Or as I like to call it, one small step for Neil Armstrong, one giant leap for Drizzle Boy. That was a space joke, I love space. People always say it's the final frontier, but it's the only frontier. We're all in space all the time. Even though in space, time doesn't matter, neither does place, or the standard rules of engagement. It just is.

Rule number two: You will be warned when there's gonna be a loud noise. Like this.

> *There is a countdown to an alarm.*

Or some harsh lights, like this.

> *The warning for harsh lighting is shown. The alarm briefly goes off, he stops it.*

Rule number three: Any time someone tries to touch me and I don't want them to, that alarm will go off. Phone? Pocket. Bag?

> BAPHOMET *appears, he has a backpack, which he begrudgingly hands over. He berates the audience.*

BAPHOMET: What the fuck are you looking at? Fuck you! And fuck you!

BAPHOMET *exits.*

DRIZZLE BOY: Thank you, Baff. That is Baphomet, but more on him later.

DRIZZLE BOY *picks up Space Bear.*

This is Space Bear. You might think a full-grown man with a stuffed toy is weird, but he helps me. And hey, some people knit macramé owls, others do Crossfit, some do meth so let's not judge the bear. Rule four I will make very clear now, so that you don't even think about breaking it. First and final warning. Rule number four is: You do not touch Space Bear. Ever.

[*To Space Bear*] You ready? Let's do this.

HOW MUCH DOES A POLAR BEAR WEIGH

DRIZZLE BOY *is plunged into uni. We hear the buzz of students, vehicles, and general ambient noise.*

STUDENT: [*voiceover*] Oi mate, you lookin' to buy some party favours? Oh, where are you goin'!?

STUDENT: [*voiceover*] Would you like to join the Campus Christian Club?

STUDENT: [*voiceover*] Hey, watch where you're going! Weirdo.

As he navigates the space, voices become louder, lights flash brightly to stop him in his tracks or turn him away. He pulls out a map of the campus, but it is no help. He gets more and more frantic as this goes on until he slumps to the ground, trying to calm himself and drown out the cacophony of stimulation. He takes out Space Bear. Pause. JULIET *appears.*

JULIET: You okay?

Everything stops. The colours of JULIET's *voice softly wash over everything.*

Are you lost? I got lost too, this place is a nightmare. Oh, you got a map. Can I?

He hands her the map. She studies it.

I'm heading to physics, room two-oh-three-A which from the number starting with a two I thought was going to be on the second—But then I realised that the two is actually a seven and someone's used a weird font. Are you going to Physics as well?

He nods.

Brilliant. If we go now we'll only be a few minutes late.

She gives him a hand up. They make their way to class. The lecturer is HANS ASPERGER.

HANS: Alright class, willkommen. I will be your lecturer for the semester, you may call me Hans.

DRIZZLE BOY: [*to Space Bear*] Are people staring at you? I feel like they're staring.

He hurriedly puts Space Bear away.

[*To Space Bear*] Sorry.

HANS: This is a momentous occasion for you all. Your first day at university. The trepidation in the air is … delicious.

DRIZZLE BOY: [*aside*] That clock is five minutes slow.

HANS: Here you begin to forge who you are into who you wish to be.

DRIZZLE BOY: [*aside*] Why is the clock slow?

HANS: The words you use, the actions you take, und the choices you make will forever seal dein Schicksal. Your fate.

DRIZZLE BOY: [*aside*] It's getting hot in here, it's making my skin itch.

HANS: This is physics, where you will learn about the very forces that control the universe in which we find ourselves so delicately placed.

DRIZZLE BOY: [*aside*] I should've brought my headphones. I left them at home.

HANS: By the end of this class, you should have a much firmer grasp of which powers are beyond your control, und the very few that are within it.

DRIZZLE BOY: [*aside*] I completely missed all of what he said, I wasn't paying attention. Pay attention.

HANS: A fun fact about me is that my favourite poem is 'Das Mädchen unter der Laterne'. Now it is your turn! Share some fun facts about yourself, tell a joke, mingle! Hingehen.

> HANS *busies himself organising assignment sheets.* JULIET *and* DRIZZLE BOY *share a look.*

JULIET: Is it just me, or is that lecturer super-weird? Or is that mean to say, it's not because he's German—I'm not—I love schnitzels. I'm Juliet, by the way. I probably should've introduced myself earlier. Call me Julie though, everyone calls me Julie. What's your name?

DRIZZLE BOY: Drizzle Boy.

JULIET: Huh. Interesting name.

DRIZZLE BOY: It's something my dad came up with.

JULIET: Well it's nice to meet you, Drizzle Boy. I'm studying a bachelor of applied science, and thinking of focusing on microbiology—

> *Pause.*

Are you okay? You look a little nervous.

DRIZZLE BOY: I am a bit. I don't do so well with new people, and I think I would honestly rather cut my fingers off than tell you five fun facts about myself—That should've been an inside thought—

JULIET: I'll go first then. Fun facts, fun facts …

HANS: Look at you all, it is beautiful! Physics at work! One of the most easily observable laws of physics is that opposite charges will be drawn to one another.

JULIET: I had toast for breakfast … which isn't a very fun fact.

HANS: Even if they are not close to each other.

JULIET: I named my car Suzanne.

HANS: Or touching.

JULIET: She's a Suzuki Swift.

HANS: This is widely known as the law of attraction.

JULIET: I like art galleries, and I'm an amateur music theatre performer, mostly because I suck at dancing too much to be a professional one.

DRIZZLE BOY: Art galleries are cool.

JULIET: Yeah? What kind of art do you like?

DRIZZLE BOY: I like—Um, sci-fi concept-arty kinda stuff? Space is very cool.

JULIET: I love space!

The colour of nervous excitement bleeds into the world.

Maybe we can go to the museum together or something?

DRIZZLE BOY: Yes! Absolutely yes. Yeah.

JULIET: Okay, sweet.

DRIZZLE BOY: Do you have friends here?

JULIET: A couple, yeah. Well, one more now.

DRIZZLE BOY: Me? You wanna be friends?

JULIET: Sure, why not?

Pause.

DRIZZLE BOY: I think I love the fun facts game.

JULIET: What are your other fun facts then?

DRIZZLE BOY: Um … my favourite star is Fomalhaut, which is a class-A star that's about twenty-five lightyears from the sun, my hero is Valentina Tereshkova, a Russian cosmonaut who was the first woman to ever go into space. Once I've finished this course I want to get a masters degree, which I'll use to get a job for my two years' relevant work experience with either NASA or JAXA, which is the Japanese Aerospace Exploration Agency. Then it's a simple matter of learning Japanese, passing the physical exam, completing ten months of intensive training, and surviving the rocket launch. Oh, and I'm autistic.

HANS: Of course, two positive or two negative charges will be thrust away from one another.

JULIET: You're on the spectrum.

DRIZZLE BOY: Yeah.

JULIET: I never would have known.

HANS: The size of the force being proportional to the value of each charge.

JULIET: I mean, you act so normal.

HANS: The more energy the individual atom has …

JULIET: You don't even look autistic.

HANS: The greater the push away from one another.

JULIET: That's not good to say, is it?

HANS: The law of repulsion.

DRIZZLE BOY: At least you caught yourself.

JULIET: Yeah, but it still feels like a little bit of a dick move on my part—Sorry I said dick. Not that I have anything against—You're really normal—That's not what I meant, I'm not saying autistic people are weird—Ah, sorry, I—I'm gonna go mingle.

> *Exit.*

> DRIZZLE BOY *takes out Space Bear.*

DRIZZLE BOY: [*to Space Bear*] Oh God, am I messing this up? [*To the audience*] This happens sometimes when I try to make friends, they feel like they have to go the extra mile, but then freak out, and disappear in a puff of anxious smoke. And I'm left sitting there awkwardly. At least I'm sitting here awkwardly with you.

HANS: Who could forget Einstein's Special Theory of Relativity? In which time runs differently depending on relative motion. Time und space become merged into what we imaginatively call …

HANS *and* DRIZZLE BOY: Spacetime.

DRIZZLE BOY: [*to the audience*] Rule number five: All the time is all the time, and time is stupid, and therefore we'll do flashbacks, flash-forwards, and even flash-sideways if I feel like it.

HANS: In this theory, time is also a coordinate.

> *Exit.*

DRIZZLE BOY: [*to the audience*] Not-so-fun fact: my life is a series of spacetime coordinates in which people either don't stick around, or they try to 'fix' me.

PURITY

Right Ascension 21 Hours, 2 Minutes, 56 Seconds. Declination 18°, 27'16".

Age ten.

Enter MOTHER, *with bleach.*

MOTHER: Sweetheart, I need you to drink this.
DRIZZLE BOY: You want me to drink bleach?
MOTHER: Yes.
DRIZZLE BOY: No. [*Aside*] Rule six: Don't drink bleach.
MOTHER: It'll be good for you.

> *He takes the bleach and reads.*

It's supposed to clear out all the toxins —
DRIZZLE BOY: Guaranteed to remove stains—
MOTHER: And bodily imperfections—
DRIZZLE BOY: Kills ninety-nine-point-nine-nine percent of germs—
MOTHER: / And cures autism!
DRIZZLE BOY: / And cures autism?
MOTHER: It's meant to fix you.
DRIZZLE BOY: And then I'll be 'normal'.
MOTHER: Yes!
DRIZZLE BOY: No.
MOTHER: No?
DRIZZLE BOY: I just don't think it's a fantastic idea to be drinking bleach.
MOTHER: Well it's not an exact science. I know.
DRIZZLE BOY: Well considering most people use it to clean mould from the kitchen sink, it's hardly fucking science at all.

> *Enter* FATHER.

FATHER: Don't speak to your mother like that!

DRIZZLE BOY: You do realise what's in this, right?
FATHER: Bleach I imagine.

Pause.

MOTHER: Sweetheart, we're just trying to help you.
FATHER: We've tried everything else.

Pause.

DRIZZLE BOY: Why don't you drink it?

He pours them each a glass of bleach.

FATHER: Excuse me?
DRIZZLE BOY: I mean, to show me that it's safe.

He hands them the glasses.

There's no harm in you drinking it, because you don't have any toxins in your body. Right, Mother?

They consider, then drink their bleach. They die.

[*To the audience*] There is a real school of thought that suggests administering bleach will cure your children of autism. Google it. Or don't, it's pretty horrific. Of course, most of that didn't actually happen.

They rise up once again. Exit FATHER *and* MOTHER.

Mum did try to get me to drink a new 'medicine' that contained bleach thanks to her work friend, Kate. 'Aunty Kate', who showed her a video about it online. But I get it, back here—Mum and Dad, they were desperate. At the time I only ate strawberry-jam toast, Hawaiian pizzas, and frozen blueberries. And I had just, um … Ah—

Pause.

After the bleach incident, I hid in my room and didn't come out for a few days. But I like this version better, it's a bit more fun. You gotta laugh at this stuff. It's better than the alternative.

HOW MUCH DOES A POLAR BEAR WEIGH PART TWO

DRIZZLE BOY *is once again in his lecture room.*

DRIZZLE BOY: [*to the audience*] A non-exhaustive list of other ways my parents have tried to 'fix' me:
One: they tried me on just about every antidepressant under the sun even though I told them that's not what I needed. The drugs made me very …

He stares lethargically into the middle distance for a good while.

Two: they made me eat three bananas every day for a year.

He takes out a banana and eats it.

ATTENBOROUGH: [*voiceover*] Here, we see a young male autist in his prime, as he takes part in his daily snacking ritual, using his powerful jaws to eat a banana.

DRIZZLE BOY: I'm still not quite sure what that was meant to do other than make me extremely regular.
Three: Acting classes to 'get me out of my shell'. To be, or not to be. That is the question. Actually, I have several questions, the main one being why does every rehearsal room smell like sweaty feet?
And four: They tried an exorcism.

He is momentarily possessed by a demonic entity. It quickly disappears.

Which was … yeah, that was a thing.

Enter JULIET. *He puts away Space Bear.*

JULIET: Hey again. Sorry about before, I—Conversations with these people are hard—One guy asked me if I had an OnlyFans, and I think he meant that as a compliment. But then the girl he was sitting with offered me some kind of Bulgarian cheese that I swear was moving—You know, you might be the most normal person here.

DRIZZLE BOY: Ah, thank you?

JULIET: You sure you're autistic? You seem pretty high-functioning if you are. Is it Asperger's?

DRIZZLE BOY: Asperger's actually isn't a term that's used any more, it's just autism.

JULIET: So are you one of those people that can remember the back of cereal boxes and stuff?

DRIZZLE BOY: Well it's more like a colour palette than a linear thing—

JULIET: That was a joke, I was joking. I dunno how to tell jokes, is it hot in here?

DRIZZLE BOY: And functioning labels aren't really a thing either.

JULIET: Oh shit, sorry. I've got no idea. I have a friend, from *Phantom*—

Beat, she expects him to know.

—*of the Opera*, whose cousin is on the spectrum but he's nothing like you, he kind of doesn't respond. Are you going to cancel me?

DRIZZLE BOY: There's a saying that goes if you've met one autistic person, you've met one autistic person.

JULIET: I like that, that's nice. You're nice. I said nice twice. Do you know anywhere I could learn this stuff? Educate don't segregate, right? I got you.

Tries to wink.

That was a wink. I can't really wink. What about Autism Talks?

DRIZZLE BOY: Noooo they are B-A-D bad.

Re-enter HANS, *who hands them papers. The anxiety of* JULIET *and* DRIZZLE BOY *grows with each added task.*

HANS: Hot off the printer, your first assignment, a three-thousand-word essay on the laws of motion, due in a week. Study notes on the conservation of mass und energy for our first quiz next lesson. Und the outline of this unit's major assignment: the practical application of physics within the modern world. Do you understand what I mean by that?

JULIET: You mean something like the way radiotherapy lasers or a solid state drive works.

HANS: Um … Ja, that—That would work.

JULIET: Easy. And—Just checking—Are we using Harvard or APA as the citation system for this unit? Oh, and would you like references as appendices or will footnotes be fine?

HANS: Harvard, und footnotes are acceptable.

JULIET: Awesome. I'm gonna go to my next class. It was nice meeting you.

DRIZZLE BOY: Oh, before you go. How much does a polar bear weigh?

She shrugs.

Enough to break the ice. It was nice meeting you too.

She smiles, then exits. Pause. He takes his assignments and goes to exit.

[*To Space Bear, in his backpack*] Could've gone worse.

HANS: You are doing well, extraordinarily so.

DRIZZLE BOY: Oh, sorry, talking out loud. Don't mind me—

HANS: A feature of your autistic psychopathy no doubt.

DRIZZLE BOY: My psychopa—What?

HANS: I am Johann Freidrich Karl Asperger. A pleasure.

DRIZZLE BOY: Except he died in 1980, so … Are you making fun of me?

HANS: Not at all. I was merely admiring the fact that you have progressed to university studies. It's amazing. Not many of your kind do.

DRIZZLE BOY: What's so amazing? I'm all over the place, I haven't answered any questions, or done any learning yet.

HANS: But you are here, you are present. Your usefulness levels are incredible, even more so once you gain the knowledge that I have to impart. Und you made a friend. A successful first day, wouldn't you say?

DRIZZLE BOY: I suppose so. What happened to the proper lecturer by the way?

HANS: They were … indisposed. Let me study you.

HANS *goes to touch* DRIZZLE BOY, *as he does, a massive alarm and warning lights go off. They stop when* HANS *retreats.*

What was that?

DRIZZLE BOY: Happens when people I don't like touch me.

HANS: Why would you not like me?

DRIZZLE BOY: You're a Nazi sympathiser who championed 'race hygiene'.

HANS: Are you saying it is bad to be hygienic?

DRIZZLE BOY: Forced sterilisation.

HANS: Suggested sterilisation.

DRIZZLE BOY: You also tortured and killed a lot of disabled kids. Which people somehow forget whenever they talk about you.

HANS: Ja, okay, that one makes me look like a bad guy. What is your name?

DRIZZLE BOY: Call me Drizzle Boy.

HANS: Drizzly Boy.

DRIZZLE BOY: Drizzle—

HANS: Drizzly B—

DRIZZLE BOY: Drizzle—

HANS: Drizzly Junge.

> HANS *hands him a very thick book. The world flushes with the colour of a ticking clock, a clattering keyboard, and a rapid heartbeat.*

I want you to lead the required reading discussion for next lesson. We will be talking about the laws of motion und how they apply to contemporary science. It's only one thousand, one hundred pages, happy reading! Und don't forget to think about those assignments. Auf weidersehen.

> *Exit* HANS. DRIZZLE BOY *takes out Space Bear, and worries himself into a mild frenzy over his assignments.*

EVENT HORIZON

The world falls away. We are in a space both beautiful and terrifying, an uncertain place of no time, and no limits. DRIZZLE BOY *breathes.*

SEAGULL OF VOSTOK 6

He is in the library. TERESHKOVA *enters, she is a formidable woman in a cosmonaut suit with medals all over her person.*

TERESHKOVA: Why are you moping?

> *He quickly puts Space Bear away.*

DRIZZLE BOY: Oh, oh my God, you're Valentina Tereshkova!
TERESHKOVA: Da.
DRIZZLE BOY: It's such an honour to meet you ma'am. Comrade? No— That's a little—
TERESHKOVA: You are like tiny mouse.
DRIZZLE BOY: Squeak?
TERESHKOVA: You think I am joking?
DRIZZLE BOY: No, just a bit frazzled—Sorry— You're amazing, and an inspiration, and should probably be in Russia.
TERESHKOVA: I will go where I wish.
DRIZZLE BOY: Evident. You're Valentina Tereshkova. The first woman to ever go into space. I'd love to go to space. Can I help you?
TERESHKOVA: Unlikely.

> *She examines him.*

DRIZZLE BOY: [*aside*] Tereshkova's been my hero ever since I was nine, and I saw a documentary about her. I always thought she was a super-intense-looking person, and ah … yeah, that checks out.

> *She examines his assignment.*

TERESHKOVA: What bullshit are you reading?
DRIZZLE BOY: Oh that's—I've only just got it, y'know?
TERESHKOVA: You wish all this to be easier. You do not want fear. Anxiety. Doubt.
DRIZZLE BOY: Yes, actually.
TERESHKOVA: Too bad.

DRIZZLE BOY: You're intelligent, and strong, and brave! What do you do when you're nervous?

TERESHKOVA: I don't read books. Let me guess. You feel butterflies becoming whirlwind in your stomach?

DRIZZLE BOY: Yes.

TERESHKOVA: Digest them.

DRIZZLE BOY: Sorry?

TERESHKOVA: No! Do not be sorry! Digest them! You think I did not feel fear when I launched into space? That I was not terrified of floating off into the vast darkness, to be swallowed by ravenous star, or torn apart molecule by screaming molecule as my form was sucked into the gaping maw of black hole? No. One is brave because they feel fear, and they overcome it regardless.

DRIZZLE BOY: Be scared. But do it anyway.

TERESHKOVA: For your major assignment, you should build rocketship.

DRIZZLE BOY: A model? Yeah that could be—

TERESHKOVA: Not model. Real, working craft, something with prochnost.

DRIZZLE BOY: How am I supposed to—

TERESHKOVA: I will bring you parts. What is better application of physics than to launch person into space? You said you wish to go there. Do it.

DRIZZLE BOY: I could just … go? Yeah … I could build a rocket. I could go to space.

TERESHKOVA: Louder!

DRIZZLE BOY: I could build a rocket.

TERESHKOVA: You could? No! You will!

DRIZZLE BOY: I will build a rocket!

TERESHKOVA: Yes!

She throws some papers to him.

The original plans to Vostok Six. See? You are less like mouse already.

Exit.

CAT'S IN THE CRADLE

DRIZZLE BOY *begins reading. Enter* FATHER, *who throws a football at his son, who tosses it back as soon as he is able.*

FATHER: Heads up! What have you got there, champ?

DRIZZLE BOY: I'm learning how to build a rocket.

FATHER: Jeez, you've already started rocket science? What's next, brain surgery?

DRIZZLE BOY: That's a different course.

FATHER: How's your first week been, mate?

DRIZZLE BOY: It was okay.

FATHER: Okay is good!

> *He goes for hug, the alarm goes off. He opts for a hand on the shoulder instead.*
>
> FATHER *gets up and plays with the football.*

Dad to Beckham. Beckham's got it. His blond tips pass one. Pass two. He goes for the top corner. And GOAL! Still got it 'aven't I?

DRIZZLE BOY: No.

FATHER: Did you ah—Meet any girls or ... ?

DRIZZLE BOY: Ah, well—No. Not yet.

> *Enter* JULIET *with two wraps.*

JULIET: I'm hungry.

DRIZZLE BOY: Although ...

FLORIOGRAPHY

Right Ascension 9 hours, 55 minutes, 52 seconds. Declination +17°, 18', 35".

Age eighteen.

JULIET: Not quite at the point of being hangry yet—Let's hope we don't get there—But I bought two wraps—ten-dollar EFTPOS minimum— Do you want one? You're not gluten-free or lactose intolerant, are you?

> *He takes a wrap.*

DRIZZLE BOY: Just autistic. Why's it green?
JULIET: They put spinach in it.
DRIZZLE BOY: I like green. [*Aside*] Green is the colour of my voice.
JULIET: You know, I have this friend—From *Merrily*—

> *Beat, she expects him to know.*

—*We Roll Along.*
DRIZZLE BOY: Good for you, that's nice.
JULIET: And she thinks you're pretty handsome.
DRIZZLE BOY: She does?
JULIET: 'Cause some people are hot, or cute—Not that you're not. But yeah, I think she'd say handsome.
DRIZZLE BOY: Oh I don't know about that—
JULIET: What would it take for her to get a date with you?
DRIZZLE BOY: That's impossible—Oh um, a date?
BAPHOMET: [*voiceover*] You don't want to do that.
DRIZZLE BOY: Never technically been on a date. I—I—I guess I'd like to get to know her first. Maybe talk a bit as friends before we … date.
JULIET: Could she give you some flowers?
DRIZZLE BOY: Flowers?

> *She hands him a book on floriography.*

JULIET: Flowers say a lot, they have a whole language. We've started learning about them in Biology one-oh-two-C, but I kind of prefer the poetic side of floriculture. Get that from my dad. Do you have a favourite flower? Mine's a frangipani. Which is a bit of a bold choice.

DRIZZLE BOY: Why?

JULIET: They're kind of related to sex and fertility. But also grace, wealth, and perfection—Not that I'm sexy, or perfect, and I'm not rich. Or fertile … all of that together makes me sound like a bag of potting mix. What's yours?

DRIZZLE BOY: Anemones.

JULIET: What do they mean?

DRIZZLE BOY: [*reading*] 'In a lot of cultures around the world anemones are seen as omens of sickness or ill-tiding. In the Victorian language of flowers they mean "you have forsaken me".' Well, I still think they're beautiful.

JULIET: I think they're handsome.

Exit JULIET. FATHER *tosses the football back to his son, pulling him from the memory.*

CAT'S IN THE CRADLE PART TWO

DRIZZLE BOY: Actually I did.

FATHER: I knew you'd be a ladies' man, just like me when I was your age. You're gonna meet a lot of girls at uni, I reckon.

Pause.

Y'know, it occurred to me that we never had the ah … the talk.

DRIZZLE BOY: Oh, oh don't.

FATHER: When a man—

DRIZZLE BOY: No seriously, don't.

FATHER: And a woman. Fall in love, or get very drunk, or are drawn together after a near death experience rescuing a malfunctioning nuclear submarine in Arctic waters, they engage in what is known as sex—

DRIZZLE BOY: Nuclear submarine?

FATHER: James Bond movies, mate, watch them, they're educational. I'd even give *A View To Kill* three stars.

DRIZZLE BOY: [*aside*] Dad gives pretty much every film three stars. He always gives one star for effort, a second for having an actor he recognises, and a third if the DVD doesn't skip.

FATHER: Whenever ol' Double-Oh-Seven is on a mission, he always finds a way to get shaken, not stirred if you know what I mean?

DRIZZLE BOY: Not really.

FATHER: That's a line he—James always shows the girl he knows how to use his goldfinger. Wink, wink, nudge, nudge, that's what she said.

> *Beat.*

I can see you're not getting it, he takes his penis—

DRIZZLE BOY: Dad! Stop it, please.

FATHER: What is it? I know these things can be embarrassing—

DRIZZLE BOY: No, I don't need the sex talk, Dad. Because I'm fairly certain everything you learnt about sex comes from movies starring Sean Connery.

FATHER: He was a wise man. And the best Bond by far. You can keep your Darren Craig or whatever his name is.

> DRIZZLE BOY *realises he has been holding the football this whole time, and tosses it back at* FATHER.

When I was your age, I was doing three things. Drinking with my mates, playing footy, and getting caught in penis flytraps.

DRIZZLE BOY: Dad!

> *Enter* MOTHER. *Throughout the following,* DRIZZLE BOY *gets into a doctor's costume.*

MOTHER: No! You can't have sex! [*To* FATHER] I sent you out here to do one thing, check in with your son, to see if he's got any concerns. And you've gone and turned it into *Love Island*—

FATHER: Well, I am concerned I never see him getting any puss. I never see you getting any, mate.

MOTHER: That's not something we should be talking to him about. Aunty Kate warned me, once you turned eighteen—

FATHER: Is it puss? Or pussy?

MOTHER: Is this what you've been teaching him?

FATHER: Not sure what the PC term is these days.

MOTHER: Please don't tell me you're learning from pornography!

FATHER: I haven't shown him any yet.

MOTHER: And you won't! The porn people are monsters. It's all fake anyway, no woman acts like that during sex.

FATHER: Porn's fake?

MOTHER: We'll talk about it later. I swear, your movies with all the sex, and violence—

FATHER: Fights build character. He should learn how to box.

MOTHER: He can't play sport.

FATHER: He could be Rocky Balboa! Four-star film.

MOTHER: He could fall over and snap his neck, is that what you want?

FATHER: I could be his Mickey Goldmill, granted without the alcoholism.

MOTHER: He's not drinking. You're not, are you?

FATHER: He could have a beer with his old man.

MOTHER: No! That's a slippery slope to taking hard drugs!

FATHER: [*aside to* DRIZZLE BOY] If you do want something a bit harder, I know a guy who could get us some reefer.

MOTHER: Pretty soon you'll be smoking, injecting heroin, and buying Nurofen Zavance even though you don't have a headache!

FATHER: Ah, whatever!

MOTHER: Whatever you do—

FATHER: / Take some risks!

MOTHER: / Just stay safe!

Pause.

DRIZZLE BOY: [*aside*] As you can see … Mum and Dad don't really deal with the idea of me being my own person, they never have. Not since the diagnosis.

PROTOSTAR

Right Ascension 15 hours, 43 minutes, 3 seconds. Declination 10°, 56', 0.6".

Age five.

DRIZZLE BOY *makes himself comfortable.* MOTHER *and* FATHER *ready themselves for the diagnosis.*

DRIZZLE BOY: So he's all squared away in the playroom?

MOTHER: Yes, he found a *National Geographic* magazine. Happy as Larry.

DRIZZLE BOY: Please, make yourselves comfortable and we'll go through the results.

> *They sit nervously opposite him. Pause.*

When I last spoke to your son, I asked him if he knew about his struggles with eye contact. Do you know what his response was? You have a very nice tie. Now, I appreciate that my tie is fucking glorious, however this is emblematic of the way he interacts with the world. For example, you might look at the night sky and see millions of stars. He looks at the sky and sees HD one-eight-nine-seven-three-three-B, a planet where it rains glass. He sees specific places, rich with meaning. A wholly different perspective, because he is autistic.

> FATHER *is silent, deep in thought.*

MOTHER: And what does that mean? Is he okay? Can we fix it?

DRIZZLE BOY: It's not like he's got cancer of the nutsack.

MOTHER: Well, he'll grow out of it, right?

DRIZZLE BOY: No, he won't grow out of it, it's how he is. And life may be tricky, but with support and people who actually care, he'll be fine.

MOTHER: Does—Does this mean we have to put him in a special school? Or—Or—Will there be medication? I'm not—Do you have a pamphlet or something we could—

DRIZZLE BOY: Are you alright?

FATHER *says nothing.*

MOTHER: Hey, are you with us?

FATHER: Is that why he doesn't like playing football with me?

MOTHER: What? Football? That's what you're—We've just found out our son's never going to be quite normal and you—

DRIZZLE BOY: And what is normal? There's no reason why he won't be able to do anything he sets his mind to. Life's a progression, it isn't a linear thing, and indeed, no two people are the same. All a diagnosis does is help you explain why he may do or not do certain things. Autism is just a different way of being. The sooner you learn that, the sooner you can stop the self-pity, and love your son.

FATHER: Love him? He's our son. We're always gonna love him.

MOTHER: Do we need to get him a helmet?

FATHER: No, he doesn't like things on his head. He won't even wear sunglasses in summer.

DRIZZLE BOY: I realise that none of that is what the doctor would have actually said to you, but I was busy in the other room reading about a Southeast Asian primate called the tarsier, so I filled in the gaps.

FATHER: Thank you, you've given us a lot to think about.

He shakes hands with DRIZZLE BOY. *Exit.*

Beat.

MOTHER: Excuse me, doctor. I know you must be incredibly busy but—

DRIZZLE BOY: I imagine you have a lot of questions.

MOTHER: Is he going to be able to live his life? Will he get a job, or start a family? I—I—And what about all the things he might miss out on? Will he leave home? Will he fall in love?

DRIZZLE BOY: I'm afraid I don't have a crystal ball.

MOTHER: But is there anything we—That I can do? I just want my son to be okay.

DRIZZLE BOY: What did you really want to ask back here, Mum?

Pause.

MOTHER: Would I be a bad mother if I left?

DRIZZLE BOY: That's a question for yourself.

MOTHER: Forget I asked that, that's horrible.

DRIZZLE BOY: There are people you can talk to. Therapists for you, or family sessions if you'd like.

MOTHER: I would like that.

DRIZZLE BOY: Now, I know this can be a difficult time. But please try and refrain from going to Doctor Google—

MOTHER: Google!

> *The* SPEAKER *appears.*

Can autism be cured?

SPEAKER: While there is no known cure for autism, there are a number of strategies you can adopt.

MOTHER: Will an autistic child put stress on your marriage?

SPEAKER: Autism Talks recommends you and your partner have a period of mourning, for the loss of the child that could have been.

MOTHER: Can autistic people make friends?

SPEAKER: While friendships are not impossible, autistic people often find connections and romantic relationships challenging. After all, who wants to love a Drizzle Boy?

> *The* SPEAKER *disappears. Exit* MOTHER. *The stage is tinged with the colour of loneliness. Pause.* DRIZZLE BOY *dismisses the* DOCTOR *role, and with it the construction of the past. Silence.*

I CAN MAKE YOU A MAN

DRIZZLE BOY: [*to the audience*] I feel I should take the opportunity to tell you that I've been thinking a lot about women lately. Which sounds really weird when I say it to you like that. It might shock you to learn that I don't have a whole lot of experience with that sort of thing. Only three instances really spring to mind.

One: Third grade when Laura Blair said her friend Amy Bourke had a crush on me. Amy Bourke was cute even though she had braces, so I went and asked her if she wanted to spend recess together, and all the other girls laughed and made gagging sounds. Which was hurtful.

Two: Michelle Graham last year, she invited me to a party, and we had sex in her car. It was really nice and roomy in there—2020 Hyundai Sonata, fairly affordable car, not bad on fuel—But I can only remember thinking two things—One: this is awesome. And two: a leather interior might look sexy, but it's very warm, and sticky, and makes a lot of really annoying creaking noises.
Three: The Year Ten formal.

Pause.

I don't want to talk about the formal. But there's this kind of want I have. To be with someone. I guess most people want that. To date, and flirt, and maybe fall in love. Not-so-fun fact only five percent of autistic people ever actually get married.

Enter JULIET.

JULIET: Would you like to get married?
DRIZZLE BOY: Jesus! Julie—

BAPHOMET *appears, bong in hand.*

BAPHOMET: And how many of them end up getting divorced?
DRIZZLE BOY: Baff, not now!
BAPHOMET: Just something to think about …

Exit.

DRIZZLE BOY: Are you proposing to me?

LOVE

JULIET: No, I was just asking—
DRIZZLE BOY: [*aside*] Do you think she can notice I'm a little frazzled?
BAPHOMET: [*voiceover*] Yep.
JULIET: I don't know how to feel about marriage. The idea of commitment is great—But it is a tool of patriarchal oppression that historically has been used to control or to barter women like cattle—

DRIZZLE BOY: [*aside*] Or that I kind of forget how to breathe and blink at the same time when she's in the room.

BAPHOMET: [*voiceover*] Hundred percent.

JULIET: Plus there's the whole idea of arguing about stupid things like cutlery, or whose turn it is to take out the bins. Relationships are hard. Harder than physics. So, you don't want to get married?

DRIZZLE BOY: Not to you—Right now—Not that I wouldn't—Not that you're not pretty—You're very pretty—Gorgeous—But I don't mean—That's not a judgement—Not trying to objectify you I swear—

JULIET: I think it would be really nice to find someone. Like it's written in the stars or something.

DRIZZLE BOY: [*aside*] Anyone else lost?

BAPHOMET: [*voiceover*] Fuck oath.

DRIZZLE BOY: [*aside*] I'm lost, and incredibly sweaty.

Pause. JULIET *produces a bouquet of flowers. A brief flash of music from* DRIZZLE BOY *'s formal. It cuts off after a moment.*

JULIET: These are for you. From me.

DRIZZLE BOY: But I thought you had a friend who—

JULIET: I was just checking. I mean, we've only really just met and— Did that come off as weird? Or was it too indirect—Sorry, I hope you like the flowers.

DRIZZLE BOY: They're stunning.

JULIET: So … ?

DRIZZLE BOY: Thank you?

JULIET: No, do you want to go out on a date?

More formal music, it cuts off after a brief moment.

BAPHOMET: [*voiceover*] You don't want to do that.

DRIZZLE BOY: [*aside*] Rule seven: Don't listen to Baphomet's rubbish advice.

[*To* JULIET] Why?

JULIET: Because I like you. Do you want my number?

DRIZZLE BOY *nods and goes to grab his phone from his backpack, causing Space Bear to fall out. He quickly puts Space Bear away and hands* JULIET *his phone.*

Oh that's cute, who's that for?
DRIZZLE BOY: It's nothing. [*To Space Bear*] I'm sorry.
JULIET: Well, there you go. Organise a date soon?

Formal music begins to creep in.

DRIZZLE BOY: Sure. A D-A-T-E date. Cool ... I haven't even been close to a date, not since, um ...

JULIET *exits. The formal hits with full force.*

WALLFLOWER

Right Ascension 11 hours, 10 minutes, 11 seconds. Declination 76°, 32', 13".

Age sixteen.

DRIZZLE BOY *is standing outside of his Year Ten formal. He has Space Bear and some flowers. Offstage we see the glimmer of lights and hear muffled music and voices from the dance.*

After a moment, there is a rumble, and an explosion of smoke and fire, BAPHOMET *appears.*

BAPHOMET: I smell someone willing to make a deal with Baphomet, lord of the shadows in your mind, the anxiety in your stomach, and that tingly feeling your get in your—Oh—Hello? Can you hear me?
DRIZZLE BOY: Leave me alone.
BAPHOMET: You want to be alone at a dance?
DRIZZLE BOY: I don't know what to do at a dance.
BAPHOMET: You could drink, talk to friends, or I dunno ... dance. But you don't really have any of that in you. Look at you.
DRIZZLE BOY: What do mean?
BAPHOMET: You brought a girl flowers, when she doesn't even know you exist.
DRIZZLE BOY: Yes she does, we're in most of the same classes.
BAPHOMET: What's her name?

DRIZZLE BOY: Grace Banks.

BAPHOMET: Banksy, right. You know what she was thinking when you tried to give 'em to her, don't you?

DRIZZLE BOY: No.

BAPHOMET: She was thinking look at this fucken idiot, brought a teddy bear to the formal.

DRIZZLE BOY: What's wrong with Space Bear?

BAPHOMET: Go home. I'll walk you.

DRIZZLE BOY: You want to hang out?

BAPHOMET: You could call it that. We can eat some shit food, listen to heavy metal …

DRIZZLE BOY: … and look at the stars? You can actually see my favourite star from here. That's Fomalhaut. It's nickname is 'the loneliest star'. It's twenty-five lightyears away from us.

BAPHOMET: Not exactly a trip down the road to the servo, is it?

DRIZZLE BOY: I should really get back to the formal.

BAPHOMET: You don't want to do that.

They watch Fomalhaut together for a while.

DRIZZLE BOY: [*to the audience*] The Year Ten formal. I'd been working up the courage to go for a whole month. Learnt all these stupid dance moves from Dad. Even borrowed 'Aunty' Kate's ex-husband's wedding suit after he eloped to Bali with his personal assistant. All I got out of it was a deal with the devil. Baphomet, my own crooked Jiminy Cricket. He introduced me to heavy metal, and he's hung around ever since. We're friends, but he does swear a lot, and want me to avoid girls, study, and the outside world as a whole. But it's better than not having anyone.

DRIZZLE BOY *goes to return to the dance.*

BAPHOMET: [*mimicking a high-schooler*] What is wrong with that guy?

DRIZZLE BOY *stops.*

[*Mimicking a different high-schooler*] Oh my god is he coming back?

DRIZZLE BOY: Stop it.

BAPHOMET *begins mimicking a series of high-school students, the intensity grows with each thought.*

BAPHOMET: Why'd he even come? Flowers won't help you get your dick wet. He tried to ask Grace on a date! Oh no, that's so sad. Stay away from me. He brought his bear as a date! Stay away from my girlfriend. Doesn't he have a carer? You think his mum helped dress him? Ew, keep him away from me! Your date wants a kiss, ya fucken special!

> *All of the high-school voices* BAPHOMET *has conjured begin to laugh.* DRIZZLE BOY *retreats from the entrance to the dance. Exit* BAPHOMET.

WONDERLAND

DRIZZLE BOY *is home after the formal, he tries to go to his room.*

MOTHER: You're back early. I thought you'd be out all night at the formal, maybe an after-party.
DRIZZLE BOY: No.
MOTHER: You've still got Grace's flowers. You didn't give them to her?
DRIZZLE BOY: She didn't want them.
MOTHER: Why not? I would've been thrilled if my boyfriend brought me flowers at the formal. What about Jono? You could still dance with your best friend.
DRIZZLE BOY: I'm going to my room.

> *He tries to go.*

MOTHER: Hang on. What's up?

> *He holds on tight to Space Bear.*

DRIZZLE BOY: I don't want to—
MOTHER: Sweetheart, did something happen with Grace?
DRIZZLE BOY: Mum, don't—

MOTHER: Did you make sure to compliment her dress like I said you should?

DRIZZLE BOY: Stop—

MOTHER: Or is it Jono? Did you two have a disagreement about which edition of *Dungeons & Dragons* is better again?

DRIZZLE BOY: No it's not like that—

MOTHER: Whatever it is, you can talk to me. I know having friends and relationships in high school is—

DRIZZLE BOY: They're not real, Mum!

MOTHER: What do you mean? You talk about them all the ti—

DRIZZLE BOY: I mean, they are real, but she's not my girlfriend, she's just a girl at school that doesn't pick on me all the time. And Jonathan isn't my best friend, he was a kid I leant a pencil to in fourth grade and he smiled at me. But that was it. We never talked, I … I lied. I lied to you and Dad about them.

MOTHER: Sweetheart, you never told us—

DRIZZLE BOY: That no-one likes me? Well they don't. I don't have anyone.

She tries to touch him, the alarm goes off.

Don't! Don't touch me.

MOTHER: It'll be okay—

DRIZZLE BOY: No! No, it won't be okay. Ever. Don't you get that?

MOTHER: Let me help. How can I fix it?

DRIZZLE BOY: By not doing anything! I didn't even want to go to the stupid formal. You made me go! It's your fault.

MOTHER: Well I'm sorry that I ruin everything for you.

MOTHER *goes to exit.*

DRIZZLE BOY: Wait.

She stops.

I shouldn't have said that to you. I should've tried to show you what was happening in my head, but I can't—So I didn't.

Exit MOTHER. DRIZZLE BOY *exits the memory.*

[*To the audience*] I don't know how to talk to people. And I think it's so unfair that I'm scared of dates, or new people, or flowers because of what other people have done to me. I'd like to take the opportunity now to tell you how I feel. But it's really—It's so hard. Because I feel … bad. And that is such a piss poor way of explaining what I feel, but I feel … bad. I feel angry. So angry. And it's no-one's fault, my fault, your fault, just because someone sitting in a skyscraper somewhere decided that I shouldn't move my hands too much, or look away from someone when they're talking, or think in colours. The world was built not welcoming of anyone but those who built it, and when others struggle to live in it, the builders have the audacity to tell those struggling that they should never have been born in the first place. Maybe … maybe I'm not mad at you. For making me an alien, an outsider, a science experiment. I'm just tired. Because it's so hard to be a full time interpreter of what people are thinking, or—Or might be thinking, but they don't say. And every time someone tries to help, it's conditional on me changing, or living by the rules that I can't follow, and it's not fair! Why can't I do it my way? Why?!

EVENT HORIZON

Silence. We are once again in that space outside of time and matter. Both enchanting and horrifying.

MOTHER: [*voiceover*] What are you doing up there?

STRUCTURAL SYSTEM

Enter TERESHKOVA, *who places a bunch of mechanical science equipment in front of* DRIZZLE BOY.

TERESHKOVA: You build.
DRIZZLE BOY: Pardon?
TERESHKOVA: Parts for your ship. For your major assignment.
DRIZZLE BOY: You brought me parts for a rocket?

TERESHKOVA: I am hearing questions and not seeing building.

DRIZZLE BOY: Oh, but I need to figure out how to actually do that, not that I'm not grateful—I don't even know if I have time right now—

TERESHKOVA: You have no time? What could be more important than building the most powerful machine known to man, hm?

DRIZZLE BOY: I have a—A date, I need to prepare. Make sure I've got witty and charming responses.

TERESHKOVA: It is mistake to date instead of work.

DRIZZLE BOY: [*aside*] Not so fun fact: I prepare a lot of things to say ahead of time. It's called scripting. And if I don't do it, sometimes I don't even know how to talk to people at all.

TERESHKOVA: Or maybe date is good. Will show you necessity of consistent work. No-one can be perfect all the time.

DRIZZLE BOY: Not even you?

TERESHKOVA: Not even me.

> *Beat.*

> If you tell anyone that I am imperfect I will crush you, malen'kiy chelovek.

DRIZZLE BOY *and* TERESHKOVA: Rule number eight: Do not fuck with Tereshkova.

> *Enter* FATHER, *with a soccer ball.*

FATHER: Hey! Whoa, what's all this?

DRIZZLE BOY: Rocketship parts.

FATHER: You didn't use your mum's credit card for this, did you?

DRIZZLE BOY: No.

FATHER: Smart move, 'cause you know how much curry I copped for ordering the Blu-Ray boxed set of *Lord of the Rings*. She didn't even care that they're four-and-a-half bloody stars.

TERESHKOVA: Who is Blu-Ray?

DRIZZLE BOY: Dad's friend.

FATHER: Do you want a hand?

DRIZZLE BOY: Do you know how to build a rocket?

> TERESHKOVA *snorts.*

FATHER: No, but I had a mate who went into space, it was him and a bunch of his crew, they were oil riggers. But NASA got 'em together 'cause of this emergency where they had to drill into this big meteor that was coming towards earth—

DRIZZLE BOY: That's the plot of *Armageddon*, Dad.

FATHER: I could still help.

TERESHKOVA: I suppose monkeys also went to space. I expect progress upon my return.

Exit.

FATHER *begins fiddling with a rocket piece.* DRIZZLE BOY *quickly stops him.*

DRIZZLE BOY: No! No, no, no, that bit there is made of gallium, which is a lightweight semiconductor that allows current to travel through it. They're components in a lot of electronics, but the reason they're important for space flight—

FATHER: So where would I put a screw in?

DRIZZLE BOY: Oh. There.

FATHER: Right.

He begins fiddling with a tiny screw on a circuit board.

Y'know, this reminds me of when you were a kid and we used to build those Lego things together.

DRIZZLE BOY: This will be one of the most intricate and complex machines that has ever been designed—

FATHER: You'd always yell at me when I made an extra bit that stuck off the side.

DRIZZLE BOY: You were compromising the structural integrity of my city.

FATHER: I was trying to make it fun, like I would have when I was a kid. Is that properly on?

DRIZZLE BOY: Looks like it.

FATHER: You know what?

DRIZZLE BOY: [*aside*] He's gonna say something about a film.

FATHER: This might be your *Rain Man* thing.

DRIZZLE BOY: [*aside*] There it is.

RAIN MAN

Right Ascension 1 hour, 46 minutes, 32 seconds. Declination +2°, 42', 2".

Age eleven.

FATHER *grabs a copy of the 1988 film.*

DRIZZLE BOY: [*to the audience*] Great movie, right? I thought so at the time, but I also got this really icky feeling. And I couldn't place why until much more recently, sort of like how the Easter Bunny is cute when you're a kid, but if you think about a seven-foot-tall human-rabbit hybrid delivering chocolate eggs as an adult, it's a little uncomfortable.

FATHER: This movie is famous for people like you. It's about an autistic bloke.

DRIZZLE BOY: What, like the actor? Is it Anthony Hopkins?

FATHER: Well I dunno—Wait? Is Anthony Hopkins autistic?

DRIZZLE BOY: Yeah.

FATHER: Huh. I just thought he was Welsh. It's Dustin Hoffman, apparently he does a damn good job. I wouldn't be surprised if he's got something in him. Google! Is Dustin Hoffman autistic question mark?

Enter SPEAKER.

SPEAKER: No.

Exit SPEAKER.

DRIZZLE BOY: [*aside*] That didn't stop Dad from getting some very strange ideas.

FATHER *takes out a flute and hands it to his son.*

FATHER: Your mum's old flute, go on, Tchaikovsky.

DRIZZLE BOY *tries, but cannot play the flute.* FATHER *grabs a French dictionary. He flips through it with blinding speed.*

Aunty Kate's French dictionary. Speed-read. Combien avez-vous mémorisé?

DRIZZLE BOY: What?

FATHER *discards the dictionary, and grabs a pencil and pad.*

FATHER: I'm thinking of six numbers between one and—

DRIZZLE BOY: Twelve, eight, three, seventeen, five and thirty-two.

FATHER *excitedly watches as the lottery is drawn, with each number drawn he becomes more dejected.*

LOTTO ANNOUNCER: [*voiceover*] Let's recap tonight's winning numbers; they are twelve, nine, twenty-four, eighteen, two, forty, and our supplementaries tonight are seventeen, and twenty-two. Well, I hope they were your winning numbers. Goodnight.

FATHER *tosses away the pencil and pad. Beat.*

FATHER: Bugger. Maybe you aren't Rain Man. Maybe you're more of a Drizzle Boy.

DRIZZLE BOY: Drizzle Boy.

They exit the flashback, and are once again building the rocket together.

FATHER: Building a rocket—Maybe we finally found your thing!

DRIZZLE BOY: Dad.

FATHER: But what about the gallium semi-erection?

DRIZZLE BOY: Semiconductor. Knowing that doesn't make me a savant, it's just basic electronics. Not everyone who's autistic is a savant, and not everyone who's a savant is autistic. That's one of the reasons I hated that film.

HOFFMAN *appears like a demented 1980s whack-a-mole.*

HOFFMAN: Hey I won an Academy Award for that role! I'm Dustin Hoffman, I can play any part I want!

DRIZZLE BOY *slams shut whatever hole* HOFFMAN *appeared from. Beat.*

FATHER: Can I still help you with the rocket?

DRIZZLE BOY: Yeah, if you want.

FATHER: We should probably shift it to the backyard. I've got a tarp to keep the rain off it.

DRIZZLE BOY: That's probably a good idea—Wait, what's the time?

FATHER: Dunno, why?

DRIZZLE BOY: I have a date.

FATHER: A date?! That's my boy!

FATHER goes for a hug, the no-touch alarm goes off.

DRIZZLE BOY: Sorry. Bit nervous.

FATHER: No, that's alright mate.

He opts for an affectionate nudge instead.

You'll have to tell me all about it. A date …

Exit.

FLIGHT CHECK

DRIZZLE BOY *continues getting ready for the date.*

DRIZZLE BOY: [*to the audience*] I want this to go well, but I'm a touch concerned that it won't. So here's a non-exhaustive list of things to talk about when it gets awkward.

One: Pets. 'So, are you a dog or a cat person?' Maybe that's not a good opening question, what if she says cats? I'm allergic, and then she'd have to choose between me or a cat, and that is a sad battle to lose.

Two: Ask her about music theatre. She said she likes musicals. But what if she says her favourite musical is *Cats*? Then I'm allergic and confused. Okay, something more esoteric.

Three: 'What's the most perfect day you can think of?' But what if her perfect day is something awful, like going to the airport. Okay—Ah—Don't panic. Panicking will make you sweaty, sweat will make you smell. Do I smell? Focus. What does she like? She likes flowers. But she said they all mean things. So if I get her the wrong ones, she might end up thinking I want to burn her house down, or sleep with her mother. I should do some research. Don't want to half arse it and seem like an idiot, or whole arse it and seem overeager. But I am eager. Maybe I should just—

BAPHOMET *appears with a heavy metal flourish.*

BAPHOMET: Ask if she wants to see your cock—

DRIZZLE BOY: 'Would you like to see my—' No! Baff, come on, she's really cool. I want this to go well.

BAPHOMET: I don't like how much time you're spending with this woman. Neither does Space Bear.

DRIZZLE BOY: But he's coming with me.

BAPHOMET: You fucking Judas.

DRIZZLE BOY: Four: I could ask her what she thinks about the James Webb telescope.

BAPHOMET: She doesn't want to hear about space, man!

DRIZZLE BOY: You don't know that! Five: I could ask about uni.

BAPHOMET: Boring.

DRIZZLE BOY: Last resort.

DRIZZLE BOY *takes Space Bear along on the date.* JULIET *enters. She and* DRIZZLE BOY *set up for their date of star-gazing.*

STAR-CROSSED

DRIZZLE BOY: So, how're you finding uni?

BAPHOMET: You're fucked.

Exit.

JULIET: Not getting lost any more.

DRIZZLE BOY: That's good. [*Aside*] I told you this wouldn't go well. [*To* JULIET] Assignments are piling up though, aren't they?

JULIET: Oh, I know! I feel like I've barely started any of them.

DRIZZLE BOY: I've only started one.

JULIET: Wait, like actually? I could help you study, if you wanted?

DRIZZLE BOY: No, no I—I'm good.

JULIET: Oh … okay.

BAPHOMET: [*voiceover*] Swing and a miss.

   Pause.

JULIET: Two guys walk into a bar, the third one was a duck—No—Shit—

DRIZZLE BOY: What?

JULIET: I messed up the punchline. It was meant to be: the third guy … ducks. 'Cause the other—They walked into the—Yeah I'm kinda nervous.

DRIZZLE BOY: Nervous?

JULIET: Yeah, because I like you.

DRIZZLE BOY: But why?

JULIET: What? Do you want me to write you a list?

DRIZZLE BOY: Maybe. [*Aside*] This is awful.

BAPHOMET: [*voiceover*] I tried to tell ya.

   Pause.

DRIZZLE BOY: [*to* JULIET] Well, it's getting kind of late—

JULIET: It is.

DRIZZLE BOY: We should probably—

JULIET: The stars are coming out.

DRIZZLE BOY: They are.

JULIET: I bought one—For my dad—A star—Did you know that's a thing? And the cheapest one's only thirty-nine ninety-five.

DRIZZLE BOY: I've been asking for one every year for Christmas.

JULIET: I did heaps of research to make sure I picked the perfect one for him.

DRIZZLE BOY: Do you know the coordinates?

JULIET: The Paul Herrington star is at right ascension ten hours, twelve minutes, nineteen seconds. And declination—ninety degrees, twenty-five arcminutes, three arcseconds.

DRIZZLE BOY: That's a nice corner of the galaxy. It's near the—

DRIZZLE BOY *and* JULIET: Octans constellation.

JULIET: You said you liked space, so I did some reading.

DRIZZLE BOY: Well … do you know what that formation is?

JULIET: Ursa Major.

DRIZZLE BOY: Spot on.

JULIET: That means big bear but most people call it—

JULIET *and* DRIZZLE BOY: The Big Dipper.

JULIET: I think it's funny that the constellations have all these weird names, 'cause they really look nothing like them. That one looks more like a spoon than a bear.

DRIZZLE BOY: Did you know there's actually never been a bear in space?

JULIET: No?

DRIZZLE BOY: Nope. They started with fruit flies in 1947, to test the effects of radiation on living organisms. Then they sent monkeys, and then mice which seems like the wrong way around in my opinion.

JULIET: Right? What would the RSPCA say?

DRIZZLE BOY: 'Stop sending animals to space.'

JULIET: [*seeing Space Bear*] Except your friend here. Hello again.

DRIZZLE BOY: [*aside*] Rule number four: Do not touch Space Bear.

JULIET: Can I see?

Pause. He retrieves Space Bear.

DRIZZLE BOY: [*to Space Bear*] What do you say? You're gonna come up sooner or later.

He shows her Space Bear.

JULIET: Oh wow!

DRIZZLE BOY: You don't think it's weird, or … ?

JULIET: No, of course not. What's their name?

DRIZZLE BOY: Space Bear.

JULIET: A bear in space. Can I?

DRIZZLE BOY: [*aside*] Rules were made to be broken.

He cautiously gives Space Bear over. She is very gentle and pleasant.

JULIET: Can you imagine real space bears? I think that'd be really cool, terrifying, but cool. Where did you get him?

COSMOS

Right Ascension 22 hours, 57 minutes, 30 seconds. Declination 29°, 37', 20".

Age six.

DRIZZLE BOY *takes* JULIET *into the memory with him. Enter* FATHER.

FATHER: You'll see, there's no eight-foot alien coming to take your skull as a trophy, I promise. It's just stars and asteroids and stuff. [*To himself*] I knew six was too young to show him *Predator*.

There is an announcement.

MUSEUM WORKER: [*voiceover*] Attention visitors, the final showing of *Solar System Sailors* will begin in ten minutes. Thank you.
JULIET: *Solar System Sailors?*
DRIZZLE BOY: Yeah, it was corny, the staff were dressed as astronauts, the seats were sticky, and the projector was humming pretty loud, making this really nasty brown colour, but it was ...
JULIET: It was what?
DRIZZLE BOY: All kinds of magic.

DRIZZLE BOY *goes into a planetarium area. The lights dim, a hush falls over the room, and a tour of the solar system begins.* DRIZZLE BOY *enters the flashback.*

SOLAR TOUR GUIDE: [*voiceover*] Hello, everyone, are you all comfortable? Strapped in? Good. I'd like to take the opportunity now, to tell you about the wonders of our universe. This is planet Earth. Everyone that has ever existed, or currently exists calls this little blue ball home. Say hello! There are seven billion people just at this moment, so remember that the next time you feel lonely. Speaking of lonely, today we're going to take a look at some of the most famous stars in the night sky. Starting with Fomalhaut, also known as 'The Loneliest Star' ...

As the narration zooms out from earth and into the stars beyond, the voice fades out. DRIZZLE BOY *is enraptured. Everything else falls away. He is floating through space, joyous and free. He talks to* JULIET *while* FATHER *plays out the flashback.*

DRIZZLE BOY: And I couldn't move. I wanted to hear it again. Five hundred more times. To know everything there was to know, and just ... give my whole heart to it.

FATHER: Come on, mate, it's time to go.

DRIZZLE BOY: Fomalhaut is also called Alpha Piscis Austrini.

FATHER: Hello in there?

DRIZZLE BOY: It emits excess infared radiation ...

FATHER: Anyone home in that head, or?

DRIZZLE BOY *does not move.* FATHER *cannot get him to.*

DRIZZLE BOY: Which tells us that it's surrounded by a circumstellar disc, that keeps everything, and everyone away.

FATHER: Mate, everyone else is gone, your mum's already waiting in the car. They're not going to play it again.

DRIZZLE BOY: Its name means 'mouth of the whale'.

FATHER: Are you alright?

DRIZZLE BOY: The spectrum of light it emits is so stable that it is used to help classify other stars when they're discovered.

FATHER: Snap out of it, will you?

FATHER *grabs* DRIZZLE BOY. *The alarm goes off, he screams and pulls away violently.*

Oh, bloody hell! Hey. I got you something from the gift shop.

FATHER *takes out Space Bear.*

But he's ... he's shy. He needs a friend. And I think he might be more comfortable if we take him home with us. Whaddya say? I mean look at him, he wants to go to space too. He's already dressed. So can we go home?

Exit FATHER, *as the memory dissolves back into the date.*

DRIZZLE BOY: And I've had him, and loved space ever since.

JULIET: You're not like other guys I've gone out with.

DRIZZLE BOY: Is that bad?

JULIET: No. Usually they just want someone to drive around in their 'super-cool' car—The last guy I went on a date with took me to the gym and told me how shit I was at deadlifts. But you're just … sweet.

> *Pause.*

You said you've never been on a date. Like, not ever?

DRIZZLE BOY: Nope. Well, nothing that I would count as one. I hung out with someone, but I don't think it was necessarily romantic.

JULIET: Just didn't go anywhere?

DRIZZLE BOY: We had sex in her 2020 Hyundai Sonata. But no romance, no.

JULIET: Well I guess if there had been, we wouldn't be here now so I should count myself lucky.

DRIZZLE BOY: I got you something.

JULIET: You did?

> *He produces some frangipanis.*

Oh thank you, they're beautiful!

DRIZZLE BOY: You are. [*Aside*] Why did I say it like that?

> *Pause.*

Are you real?

JULIET: Yeah.

> *She holds his hand.*

DRIZZLE BOY: Just checking.

> *Pause.*

Do you ever think about how everything was made out of stardust, and that all of the little bits solidified and then evolved to become us.

JULIET: So we're all made out of stars. Is that why you like space? 'Cause it makes you feel less alone?

Beat.

DRIZZLE BOY: You know, I'm building a rocket.

JULIET: Really?

DRIZZLE BOY: Well, I'm working on it. Imagine being out there. In the universe. All the light. The wonder. Space bears. I'm gonna get up there, I just know it.

JULIET: It's written in the stars?

DRIZZLE BOY: Something like that.

Pause.

You know, you could come too. If you wanted.

Pause.

Was that a yes, or … ? [*Aside*] What does that mean? Do you know what that expression means?

Exit JULIET.

ROSETTA

Right Ascension 18 hours, 40 minutes, 24 seconds. Declination 19°, 56', 31".

Age seventeen.

Enter DOCTOR.

DOCTOR: I am going to offer you a series of expressions that someone might encounter in day-to-day life. You just have to tell me what emotion corresponds to each one, that way we can avoid another misunderstanding like the formal. I've just dropped my ice cream, you feel …

DRIZZLE BOY: Not much, it wasn't my ice cream.

DOCTOR: Alright, what if we say it is your ice cream, you feel …

DRIZZLE BOY: What flavour?

DOCTOR: Sorry?

DRIZZLE BOY: What flavour ice cream? That'll change how I feel.

DOCTOR: Rocky Road—

DRIZZLE BOY: Don't like Rocky Road.

DOCTOR: The flavour is unimportant—You feel …

DRIZZLE BOY: Frustrated.

DOCTOR: Wrong, sad.

DRIZZLE BOY: Okay.

DOCTOR: My dog is greeting me as I arrive home. He is wagging his tail and giving me lots of affection, the way I feel is …

DRIZZLE BOY: Glad to be home from work?

DOCTOR: No, about the dog—

DRIZZLE BOY: What's your opinion on your dog?

DOCTOR: In real life I don't have one, so it's irrelevant.

DRIZZLE BOY: Then I should think you would be concerned that there is a dog in your house.

DOCTOR: In this hypothetical situation, I have a dog, I love it very much, and it is behaving in the manner described. The way I feel is …

DRIZZLE BOY: Joyous?

DOCTOR: Wrong. Happy. Why don't we try something else? I'm going to make a facial expression and you tell me what you see. There's no right or wrong answers. Take your time.

DOCTOR *makes a face, it is indecipherable. Beat.*

DRIZZLE BOY: Constipated?

DOCTOR: Take your time, it's okay.

DRIZZLE BOY: I don't know.

DOCTOR *makes the face again.*

Are you sure it's not constipation?

DOCTOR: Oh come on!

DRIZZLE BOY: You should eat more bananas, it'll keep you regular.

DOCTOR: It's simple.

DRIZZLE BOY: Then maybe just tell me?

DOCTOR: This is the face of someone who has just seen their ninety-year-old grandmother get hit by a car, and whilst they ran out to see if she was okay, was hit by a bus. They are now passing into the next life, seeing God and the Devil in an extended, and somewhat erotic argument about where their soul should go once they finally depart.

Pause.

DRIZZLE BOY: How the fuck am I meant to work that out?

DOCTOR: No swearing in my office!

DRIZZLE BOY: Sorry.

DOCTOR: Right. It is imperative we get on top of all this. We need to prepare you for university.

DRIZZLE BOY: Space is really the bigger goal.

DOCTOR: Let's conquer Earth before we zip off to the stars, shall we? If we don't focus and sort this out, then you'll act all … weird.

DRIZZLE BOY: Autistic?

DOCTOR: No, goodness me. What kind of person do you think I am?

DRIZZLE BOY: But I can't keep acting the way I usually do.

DOCTOR: No.

DRIZZLE BOY: Because the way I've been acting is autistic.

DOCTOR: Weird.

DRIZZLE BOY: What?

DOCTOR: Weird. You're weird.

Exit.

DRIZZLE BOY: No. I'm autistic. Motherfucker. Explosion of joy, and self-acceptance.

TRANSMITTER/RECEIVER

DRIZZLE BOY *joyfully builds his rocket. At one stage he is working with some kind of electricity, the power goes out. Blackout.*

MOTHER: [*offstage*] Oh bloody hell, not again!
DRIZZLE BOY: Sorry!

> DRIZZLE BOY *begins to fix the power.*

FATHER: [*offstage*] I was halfway through *Cool Runnings*!

> *He fixes the power.*

GUIDANCE SYSTEM

Enter HANS.

HANS: You seem stressed. Are you taking on too much?
DRIZZLE BOY: I'm fine.
HANS: Pride comes before the fall.
DRIZZLE BOY: Is there something you need?
HANS: Yes, I did stop by for a reason.
DRIZZLE BOY: Was that to be intimidating?
HANS: You think I am intimidating. Dankeschön. I have been practising. He hands over some papers. Your quiz results.
DRIZZLE BOY: But this says I—
HANS: Failed. Ja. I took marks away because you did not show your methods.
DRIZZLE BOY: But I got the answers right, that—
HANS: And still failed.
DRIZZLE BOY: No, but how can—
HANS: And what about your major assignment? Have we had any thoughts at all about that?
DRIZZLE BOY: I'm working on a demonstration of space exploration based on the launches of Valentina Tereshkova.

HANS: Tereshkova. You are aware that Putin is puttin' it in her?

DRIZZLE BOY: I'm building a rocket.

HANS: Oh mein Schatz. You would do well to think more ... realistically. For someone with your condition, I would suggest something like demonstrating static electricity with balloons.

DRIZZLE BOY: Maybe I should try something simpler—

HANS: Simple is as simple does ... or, you could simply drop out. Auf wiedersehen, Drizzly Junge.

> HANS *exits.* DRIZZLE BOY *stuffs the failed test in his bag as he tries to calm himself.*

SYNAESTHESIA

Enter JULIET.

DRIZZLE BOY: I failed our first quiz.

JULIET: Was it the question about invariant and relativistic mass? That whole section was—

DRIZZLE BOY: I got the answers correct.

JULIET: Then how did you fail?

DRIZZLE BOY: Apparently it doesn't matter if the answers are correct, it matters that you communicate you're correct in a way the university enjoys. And now I'm kind of terrified that I might fail the whole semester. But I won't, I'll just work harder ... Still not a hundred percent on why you like me. I mean, you're so clever—

JULIET: Stop!

DRIZZLE BOY: And beautiful—

JULIET: Go on.

DRIZZLE BOY: And you're really funny.

JULIET: Even though I can't land a joke.

> *He smiles.*

I like your smile. It's going on the list.

DRIZZLE BOY: [*aside*] And now I can't stop smiling.

Pause. JULIET *tries to hold his hand or connect with him in some way, he moves out of her range.*

It's nice to see you. I'm having a bit of a bad day. I cut all the tags off my shirts so they don't scratch. And there's so much of the colour yellow around today which is … upsetting.

JULIET: What's wrong with yellow?

DRIZZLE BOY: Yellow is the colour of my mum screaming. It makes my teeth itch.

JULIET: Is that an autism thing?

DRIZZLE BOY: Synaesthesia. It's not exactly an autism thing, although it is more common. For me, sounds make colours.

JULIET: And yellow sucks.

DRIZZLE BOY: Yellow is the worst.

Pause.

JULIET: Hey, what colour weighs less than blue?

He shrugs.

Light blue.

DRIZZLE BOY: That's not too bad.

JULIET: I stole it off the internet.

DRIZZLE BOY: You thief.

JULIET: Quiet music?

DRIZZLE BOY: Quiet is fine.

JULIET *puts on a rendition of 'Moon River'. It continues softly in the background. Beat.*

This is a really nice combination, lots of complementary colours, with a little bit of static from the old recording.

JULIET: That must be so cool. I wish I could see it.

DRIZZLE BOY: Close your eyes. It looks something like this. Pretty cool huh?

The music fades up, the colours of the song intensify until they are vibrant and full of life. JULIET *enjoys them for a moment. He watches her as she sings a line or two. The colours of her voice bleed into those of the song.*

She makes some joyful noises to play with the colours of her voice. She begins to dance with the music. The moves are silly, and yet very charming.

JULIET: Dance with me?

DRIZZLE BOY: I can't …

JULIET: Neither can I. I once did a production of *Cats*—They put me way at the back, I was practically in the wings.

DRIZZLE BOY: Okay.

They dance. DRIZZLE BOY *slowly gets more into it.* BAPHOMET *appears.*

BAPHOMET: Flowers, dancing? You look fucken ridiculous.

Exit.

They stop. Perhaps they fall down beside each other. It's adorable. Pause.

DRIZZLE BOY: Sorry.

JULIET: This was my favourite song when I was really little.

DRIZZLE BOY: Why's that?

JULIET: My dad. He used to play it in the car when he would pick me up from primary school. I know all the words. We'd sing the whole thing over and—He used to do this thing where he'd try and sing the soprano part, and when he did, he'd make all these funny faces … It was just—It was fun.

DRIZZLE BOY: You guys don't do that any more?

JULIET: He um—He died last year.

DRIZZLE BOY: Oh that's … You don't have to talk about it if you don't want to.

JULIET: No it's okay. He had a stroke. Mum was at work, I was at school, and he had the day off. He'd been gardening in the backyard. When I left for school, he was there. And when I got home, he wasn't.

DRIZZLE BOY: D'you miss him?

JULIET: Every day. But he's there every night. Because if he's stardust, then he's not really gone.

DRIZZLE BOY: He's not.

JULIET: The star I bought him is easier to think about, 'cause it's in one spot.

DRIZZLE BOY: He probably has space bears to keep him company.

She smiles. Pause.

I—I don't always read people the way they think I will or—Maybe the way they should be read, which is why I couldn't text you after our date. But ... I am learning, about you. What you mean, and what you mean to me ...

JULIET: You should know that I like you, a lot.

DRIZZLE BOY: I like you too. A lot.

Beat. They might kiss, but don't.

JULIET: You can so dance.

DRIZZLE BOY: I did a lot of practise for my high-school formal. [*Aside*] Dad made me watch *Dirty Dancing*—four-and-a-half stars— Multiple times. We practised the lift at the pool.

FATHER *enters, in budgie smugglers.*

FATHER: Come on, mate, nobody puts my baby in the corner ... three, two, one, jump! ... We'll go again ...

Exit.

JULIET: What's your signature move? Like, I do the frustrated bumblebee.

She demonstrates. He laughs.

What's yours?

DRIZZLE BOY: The moonwalk.

He demonstrates an accurate recreation of an astronaut walking on the moon. She laughs.

JULIET: Well that's impressive. But I believe you stole it from Neil Armstrong. What about 'oh no the fire alarm is going off'?

DRIZZLE BOY: Not bad. What about 'the Walking Dead'?

They dance together, it is joyful, intimate, and lively. The world shifts as they are transported to the moon, where they dance for a moment, until they are face-to-face. Pause. They kiss. Exit JULIET.

DRIZZLE BOY *laughs, recovering his breath, and revelling in the joy of their kiss. He is lost in the moment.*

WILFUL WELCOME

Enter MOTHER *dressed ready to go out.*

MOTHER: What's happening out here?

DRIZZLE BOY: Securing fuel lines. Don't want any explosions. [*Aside*] That would be B-A-D bad.

MOTHER: And when will I get my clothes line back? Is that my blender? You're putting a whole lot of your eggs in the space basket, sweetheart. Have you thought about any back-ups yet?

DRIZZLE BOY: Back-ups? I'm. Going. To. Space!

MOTHER: I read in your course guide that you could do statistics or pharmacology. Those are some really high-paying jobs.

DRIZZLE BOY: Please don't.

MOTHER: Don't what?

DRIZZLE BOY: Don't ruin this for me.

MOTHER: Sorry. What would I know? I've only looked after you your whole life.

DRIZZLE BOY: Well when I'm in space, you won't have to worry.

MOTHER: But it's my job to worry about you. And right now I'm worried about you not being ready.

DRIZZLE BOY: Ready for … ?

MOTHER: The party. Aunty Kate's party. We've had the invitation for almost a month now. You didn't forget, did you?

DRIZZLE BOY: Just Kate, she's not my aunt. And no, I didn't forget, I'm not going. I'm going to see Julie.

MOTHER: Who's Julie?

DRIZZLE BOY: [*aside*] Oh no … [*To* MOTHER] My girlfriend.

MOTHER: This isn't another Grace Banks situation—

DRIZZLE BOY: No, I'm not making her up.

MOTHER: We made the commitment to go to this party as a family.

DRIZZLE BOY: My name isn't on the invitation. It doesn't say I'm invited, so I'm not.

MOTHER: Oh don't be silly—

DRIZZLE BOY: I'm not.

MOTHER: Of course you're invited, they invited the family. Now come on, get ready, we gotta go.

DRIZZLE BOY: No.

MOTHER: It would mean a lot to me if you came today. We can get pizza on the way home if you don't like any of the food, and I'm sure there'll be a quiet spot—

DRIZZLE BOY: I'm not a child, Mum, you can't just bribe me with pizza, and put me in the quiet corner.

MOTHER: You're an adult now, are you?

DRIZZLE BOY: Yes, so stop getting in my business—

She shows him the failed test.

MOTHER: Well it's not very adult of you to be failing uni, and to be hiding it. You keep talking about this dream of going to space.

DRIZZLE BOY: It's not a dream. I'm building a rocket.

MOTHER: If you say so. Sweetheart, listen to me.

DRIZZLE BOY: Why? You never listen to me.

MOTHER: The first dream, or first love you have, is not necessarily going to be the one that succeeds. And if you don't buckle down, that dream of space, is just going to be that. A dream.

DRIZZLE BOY: You don't believe in me.

MOTHER: I do. But I also know that you're not like other people, you need looking after. That's all I'm doing, all I've ever tried to do.

DRIZZLE BOY: You tried to shut me up with medications.

MOTHER: They were the first thing we were told to try—

DRIZZLE BOY: Electroshock therapy.

MOTHER: Was recommended to us by—

DRIZZLE BOY: Bleach.

MOTHER: This is all your father's fault, he showed you *Rain Man*, and now you think you're superhuman.

DRIZZLE BOY: I'm not superhuman. But I am my own human, and you need to let me grow up. You need to let me go—

MOTHER: No!

Beat.

No. We can talk about this after the party, come on—

DRIZZLE BOY: I'm not go—

MOTHER: Oh for fuck's sake, can you just do this one thing?! I'll call Aunty Kate—

DRIZZLE BOY: Kate! She's not my aunty!

MOTHER: Kate—Kate! I'll call Kate and get her to tell you you're invited. All I ever do is for you, to help you. Every doctor, treatment, time I have dropped everything so that you could be safe—And happy. But do I ever get any thanks?

Pause.

God you make things hard sometimes, love. I'm sorry. I shouldn't have snapped. Are you coming, or not?

DRIZZLE BOY *shakes his head.*

Alright.

Exit.

THE WINGS OF ICARUS

Enter HANS. DRIZZLE BOY *hands him an assignment.*

HANS: Your essay is late.

DRIZZLE BOY: Rule number five: All the time is all the time and time is stupid—

HANS: Stupid? No. Time is constant. This is overdue.

Beat.

You do not seem to care.

DRIZZLE BOY: I do, I'm just—I sent you an email asking for an extension.

HANS: That is not the proper channel, you should have filed a request through the university website.

DRIZZLE BOY: How was I supposed to know that?

HANS: Perhaps we ask too much of you. Perhaps you are not ready.

DRIZZLE BOY: Not ready?

HANS: For university. For adult life. For going to space.

DRIZZLE BOY: No, I am, I swear—I am.

HANS: Perhaps we as an institution need to provide you more support. But you must admit that to me, und yourself. The major assignment is due tomorrow. Do you need help?

DRIZZLE BOY: No.

HANS: Very well. Sie verschwenden meine Zeit und therefore are a waste of space. Auf Weidersehen.

Exit.

Enter JULIET, *in a whirlwind of excitement.*

JULIET: I have something for you.

DRIZZLE BOY: Julie, I really don't—

JULIET: It's only gonna take a second.

DRIZZLE BOY: I have to go, the major assignment is due tomorrow—

JULIET: Just promise you won't laugh?

She takes out a prepared speech and reads.

A non-exhaustive list of reasons why I like Drizzle Boy. One: I love the way you think. Two: You are excellent company. Especially to Space Bear. Three: You don't judge people based on first impressions—Which is good because I was not great. Four: Your smile. Five: Your eyes are beautiful, and they sparkle when you're talking about space, or me—That's really cute by the way. Six: Your

voice—Your voice is like a weighted blanket over my worries. And
seven: I can't wait to see you fly off in your rocketship, and I have
no doubt that you will.

Pause.

So, um … Yeah.
DRIZZLE BOY: Thank you.

He goes to leave.

JULIET: Wait—Where are you going?
DRIZZLE BOY: Home. I've got to—
JULIET: But I just told you why …
DRIZZLE BOY: You like me. I know, but—
JULIET: No.
DRIZZLE BOY: No?
JULIET: It's my way of saying that I—
DRIZZLE BOY: Can we do this later? I'm—
JULIET: This is important.
DRIZZLE BOY: I'm going to miss the bus.
JULIET: Wait.
DRIZZLE BOY: What's that face?
JULIET: Nothing.
DRIZZLE BOY: Are you upset? Your voice has gone all orangey-yellow.
JULIET: It's fine. Go catch your bus.
DRIZZLE BOY: Just tell me what you're thinking.
JULIET: I did.
DRIZZLE BOY: No you didn't.
JULIET: I did
DRIZZLE BOY: You didn't. You read me a list.
JULIET: I was thinking about all the times you asked why I like
    you—I just—I was trying to tell you—It's okay. You go.
DRIZZLE BOY: Just say what you mean.
JULIET: The list—It was my way of saying I love you.

Beat. She moves to touch him. He pulls away, she stops.

DRIZZLE BOY: Don't—I can't handle it right now.

JULIET: I just want to hold your hand.

DRIZZLE BOY: There's too much pressure, I can't do this— [*Re their relationship*] and uni, and get it all—Right. No matter how hard I try—Everyone expects me to fail. So I can't. You don't get it, you wouldn't get it, but when you're autistic, you have to succeed twice as much just to prove that you can do it at all. I don't have time—

JULIET: For what? For me? I just want to be with you.

DRIZZLE BOY: I'm sorry, I just—I'm sorry, I don't know what I feel. I do feel something for you, but I don't know if it's love. I don't know what love feels like. Or is meant to feel like.

JULIET: I'm pretty sure it's not meant to feel like this.

DRIZZLE BOY: This isn't easy for me.

JULIET: And, what? It is for me?

DRIZZLE BOY: It's easier.

JULIET: It isn't easy for anyone.

Tries to reach out.

DRIZZLE BOY: Stop! Don't do that. Don't act like you feel sorry for me.

JULIET: I'm trying to help you.

DRIZZLE BOY: Well I want a girlfriend, not a fucking carer.

Beat.

I didn't mean that—

He goes to touch her, she pulls away. JULIET *exits.*

God damn it. Fuck, Julie. Come back, please.

EVENT HORIZON

We enter the dark, twisting place with no time, a strange sense of home is present. Faint sirens in the distance. DRIZZLE BOY *breathes.*

MOTHER: [*voiceover*] What are you doing up there?! You're gonna hurt yourself! Sweetheart, please!

FATHER: [*voiceover*] Just stay there! I'm gonna get you down!

PROPULSION SYSTEM

Enter FATHER *and* TERESHKOVA.

TERESHKOVA: That piece does not go there!
FATHER: Hey, mate.

DRIZZLE BOY *begins packing to go to space.*

TERESHKOVA: This is not going according to the designs. Why have you not followed the instructions?

FATHER *begins fiddling with the rocketship parts.*

DRIZZLE BOY: No, Dad, I just need—
TERESHKOVA: What is the ape doing?
FATHER: I think that bit—

FATHER *makes a clang.*

TERESHKOVA: I do not see how you have not completed this sooner. When I first launched into space, it was in tin can. USSR technology practically made from chicken wire.
DRIZZLE BOY: Well I made mine from a Nutribullet, and an alarm clock from the eighties.
TERESHKOVA: You must not be in rush, boy. These are delicate machines.
DRIZZLE BOY: I know that, but it's due in four hours—

Another clang from FATHER.

TERESHKOVA: The entire schedule must be pushed back. Delayed.
DRIZZLE BOY: Delayed? No, no, no. I need to go.
TERESHKOVA: Not until you are in your right mind.
DRIZZLE BOY: I'm going whether you like it or not.
TERESHKOVA: Rule number eight: Do not fuck with Tereshkova. Broken.
DRIZZLE BOY: Along with your integrity.

TERESHKOVA: Enough!

DRIZZLE BOY: I did some detailed reading on you.

TERESHKOVA: I will not suffer fools!

DRIZZLE BOY: Then why do you support Putin?!

TERESHKOVA: My leader wrestles bears with bare hands, he does not carry one around in backpack.

DRIZZLE BOY: Never meet your heroes.

TERESHKOVA: I cannot commit to mission I know will fail.

DRIZZLE BOY: It's not going to fail. I'm not going to fail.

TERESHKOVA: Perhaps in trying to get to space, you forget why you wanted to go in the first place. Do svidaniya.

Exit.

FATHER *breaks part of the ship.*

FATHER: Whoops.

DRIZZLE BOY: What did you do?!

FATHER: It'll go back on, just need some glue or twine—

DRIZZLE BOY: Twine? This isn't a model, Dad!

FATHER: I once had a mate who got stranded on a desert island and found his way back home on a raft he made out of bamboo and twine. Tragically he lost his best mate Wilson at sea.

DRIZZLE BOY: Life isn't a movie, Dad! I'm not Rain Man! You don't know Tom Hanks! And you cannot hold a rocket together with twine! And no, things won't magically be better if we just go and do a stupid training montage, and you say that you believe in me. I wish you'd stop acting like your life is part of a film because it's sad. It's really—Pathetic.

Pause.

FATHER: I'm … I'm sorry.

DRIZZLE BOY: Just get out.

FATHER: No, I want to make this right. Do you want to talk, or—

DRIZZLE BOY: Get out!

FATHER *goes to exit, then pauses.*

FATHER: I love you, mate.

Exit.

DRIZZLE BOY *begins to search for Space Bear. He is nowhere to be found. The longer this goes on, the more agitated he becomes.*

CATASTROPHE

DRIZZLE BOY: Excuse me—
MOTHER: [*offstage*] You're excused.
DRIZZLE BOY: Not what I meant. Where is Space Bear?
MOTHER: [*offstage*] That's actually what I wanted to talk to you about.
DRIZZLE BOY: Where is he?
MOTHER: [*offstage*] You haven't wanted or needed him in so long, I—
DRIZZLE BOY: Well I need him now.
MOTHER: He was looking a bit dirty—
DRIZZLE BOY: So?
MOTHER: I did a load of washing and …
DRIZZLE BOY: Mum?

Enter MOTHER *with a basket of washing. A destroyed Space Bear is mixed in.*

MOTHER: He was in with the towels and—I thought I put it on a gentle cycle, but … I'm sorry.

Exit.

DRIZZLE BOY *slowly goes to the basket and reveals the destroyed Space Bear. He begins to wail and weep.*

OVERLOAD

Enter DOCTOR, *whose presence is multitudinous in this scene.* DRIZZLE BOY *is getting ready for take off. The stage is flooded with harsh lighting, this changes from moment to moment. At one time it is a sea of red, drowning the space, at another, flashes of greens and yellows and bile whites blind him intermittently. The sounds of life and movement begin, they are grating, a worm in the ear, fingernails down the raw spine. A scientific hellscape.*

DRIZZLE BOY: Final check for all systems and crew.
DOCTOR 1 *and* 2: Bite down on this.
DOCTOR 2: Why do you feel like you're failing?
DRIZZLE BOY: I'm not! I cannot—
DOCTOR 1: I cannot commit to a mission I know will fail.
DOCTOR 2: The personification of the stuffed bear is rather concerning.
DOCTOR 1: This one is called Effexor, and it's to help with your low moods.
DRIZZLE BOY: This is a comms check for mission control.
DOCTOR 2: Control yourself.
DOCTOR 1: Do you experience maladaptive daydreaming?
DRIZZLE BOY: What does that even mean?
DOCTOR 2: Does scripting have something to do with your self-worth?
DRIZZLE BOY: I refuse to be a loser.
DOCTOR 1: You should know that I like you. A lot.
DRIZZLE BOY: Juliet!
DOCTOR 2: Does the bear talk to you?
DOCTOR 1: Clonazepam, for the social anxiety.
DRIZZLE BOY: All hands, we are green light for launch.
DOCTOR 1: And when did the demonic goat figure first appear?
DOCTOR 2: You brought a girl flowers when she doesn't even know you exist.
DRIZZLE BOY: I repeat, we are go for launch.
DOCTOR 2: Paliperidone, twice a day.
DRIZZLE BOY: I don't need that.
DOCTOR 1 *and* 2: Bite down on this.

DRIZZLE BOY: Launch sequence engaged.

DOCTOR 1 *and* 2: This will fix you.

DRIZZLE BOY: This will be physics in motion.

DOCTOR 2: Who could ever love a Drizzle Boy?

DRIZZLE BOY: Blast-off in T-minus ten.

DOCTOR 1: Does the goat man tell you to do things?

DRIZZLE BOY: Nine—

DOCTOR 2: Do you feel unsafe without your bear?

DRIZZLE BOY: Eight—

DOCTOR 1: Was the roof a cry for help?

DRIZZLE BOY: No. Seven—

DOCTOR 2: Your assignment is late.

DRIZZLE BOY: Six—

DOCTOR 1: Do you often feel alone?

DRIZZLE BOY: Five—

DOCTOR 1 *and* 2: Bite down on this.

DRIZZLE BOY: Four—

DOCTOR 2: Charge powering up.

DRIZZLE BOY: Three—

DOCTOR 2: You're faking your autism.

DRIZZLE BOY: Two—

DOCTOR 1: God you make things hard sometimes, love.

DRIZZLE BOY: One. Blast-off.

The rocket is failing.

Eject, eject, something's gone wrong!

The sounds continue. The rocketship is crashing, the roar of a dying jet of flame.

Abort mission!

The roar of rocket engines, a thunderous boom.

Abort!

Shrapnel zips through the space and tears the air as it goes. The rocket failure tears DRIZZLE BOY *to pieces. He is dead. Pause.*

BEYOND OBLIVION

We travel to the moment that has been replaying. The place that is both horrible and wonderful. The bottom of the black hole. The glow of a television illuminates DRIZZLE BOY, *it flicks through several channels before it lands on ...*

AUTISM TALKS: [*voiceover*] I am autism. I'm visible in your children, but if I can help it, I am invisible to you until it's too late. I know where you live. And guess what? I live there too. I don't sleep. So I make sure you don't either. If you're happily married I will make sure that your marriage fails. I will make it impossible for your family to easily attend a birthday party. Temple. Or public park. Without struggle. Without embarrassment. Without pain. I am autism. You have no cure for me. Your scientists don't have the resources, and I relish their desperation. I have no interest in right or wrong. I derive great pleasure out of your loneliness. I will fight to take away your hope, and your dreams. I am autism. I am winning. You are scared. And you should be.

      Enter MOTHER *and* FATHER.

DRIZZLE BOY: I'm ten years old, and I'm standing on the roof of our house. This ad keeps playing in my head, over and over, while I climb to the highest point I can get. I am holding Space Bear. He's soft.
MOTHER: What are you doing up there?!
DRIZZLE BOY: I am the loneliest star.
MOTHER: You're gonna hurt yourself!
DRIZZLE BOY: A freak of nature.
MOTHER: Sweetheart, please!
DRIZZLE BOY: A spastic.
FATHER: Just stay there!
DRIZZLE BOY: A retard.
FATHER: I'm gonna get you down!
DRIZZLE BOY: All the people in the neighbourhood are screaming at me to come down. Mum and Dad think I'm going to jump. I'm not. I'm just

staring out at space that's all, trying to get away from this fucking Autism Talks ad. But they all think—They all think I'm going to kill myself. And that hasn't even entered my mind, but once the thought is there, it stays. It never really goes away. I think about it a lot. I come back here often, to this moment. But if I breathe, if I turn everything down, the air is damp, the sky is clear and I can see all the way into the universe. No-one owns space, no-one can tell you how or what to be. If down here I am autism, up there I am a new star, a bright nebula, a whole galaxy of my own.

ROCKET MAN

DRIZZLE BOY *is at the bottom of the black hole. Silence. Enter* FATHER, *with some strawberry-jam toast.*

FATHER: Hey, mate, I brought you some toast, it's ah—I'll just leave it here.

> *Pause.*

You've gotta eat something.

> *Beat.*

The blueberries have gone bad, I'll toss them out.

> *Beat.*

I can make you a cuppa tea if you want?
DRIZZLE BOY: Thanks, Dad.
FATHER: That's alright. I know it's probably not as good as your mum's, think I burnt it.
DRIZZLE BOY: Mum not back?
FATHER: Ah, not yet.
DRIZZLE BOY: But she will be?
FATHER: Yeah, course. You know she can't stand Aunty Kate—Kate, for very long. Another day or two, I reckon.

> *Pause.*

She's worried that you're taking too many risks, too much on.
I think she blames herself.

Pause.

You gave it your best shot, mate. Even got a few feet in the air
before—And those blokes from fire and rescue said it was probably
the Nutribullet that did it.

DRIZZLE BOY: Sorry about the deck.

FATHER: That's alright.

DRIZZLE BOY: And the clothes line.

FATHER: We've got a dryer.

DRIZZLE BOY: Should I pay for the neighbour's fence?

FATHER: They said it needed redoing anyway.

Pause.

Do you, ah—D'you wanna talk about it?

DRIZZLE BOY: I dunno.

Pause.

FATHER: Has Juliet called you?

DRIZZLE BOY: No.

FATHER: She will. I'm sure she will.

Silence.

I'll um—I'll put the kettle on.

He goes to leave.

DRIZZLE BOY: I'm really—I'm so sorry.

FATHER: For the fence? Don't worry about it—

DRIZZLE BOY: No … For everything. For—For not being normal—For
not being the son you wanted—I'm sorry I'm a fuck-up. I'm—I'm
a failure, Dad.

He hugs his dad. Pause.

FATHER: Hey … Hey … Oh mate, you're not. Not at all.

DRIZZLE BOY: I don't think I can go back to uni. Ever.

FATHER: That's not the end of the world. There's millions of other things you could do.

They hold each other for a moment.

I never went to uni, and I turned out alright, didn't I? Got a good job, family, son who's sharp as a razor. It's not the end, you know?

Pause.

If everyone gave up when their first idea crashed and burnt, the world wouldn't work. So, you didn't make your dream come true, you can find a new one, mate. You've just got to—It's about ah— Think about what comes next. In bits and pieces. I know that's not exactly how you'd want to do it, but maybe you could go slower. Just a bit … You wanted a rocket launch. But for you every day is like a bloody rocket launch. And there's only one person that needs to be in control of that, and that's you.

Pause.

How about we watch a movie? We'll bring space to us, I just got the boxed set of *Alien*. They're great films, you'll love 'em. The first one's four-and-a-half stars. And that Sigourney Weaver, I mean, don't tell your mum but who—ah. She's phenomenal. A real movie hero.

DRIZZLE BOY *says nothing. Pause.*

But you … you're—Ah, you're my hero—Watching you has been better than any movie. You're five stars, mate.

Pause. Exit FATHER.

EXORCISM

BAPHOMET*'s physical body has been dispelled, he continues via a voiceover.*

BAPHOMET: [*voiceover*] It's all fucken blown up in your face, hasn't it? You've got nothing.

DRIZZLE BOY: Yes I do.

BAPHOMET: [*voiceover*] You need me, so let me help.

DRIZZLE BOY: No.

BAPHOMET: [*voiceover*] Come on, we'll go have a drink, pull a cone, fuck off with all this self-actualising shit.

DRIZZLE BOY: I'm not sixteen any more. And we both know you came from the artwork on a heavy metal album cover. I made you up.

BAPHOMET: [*voiceover*] But our friendship—

DRIZZLE BOY: Is over.

> BAPHOMET *disappears into the void of the black hole. Silence.*

Goodbye Baff.

> *Beat.*

[*To the audience*] I feel I should take the opportunity now to tell you I will never make it to space.

> *Beat.*

And that's okay.

> *Enter* MOTHER.

MOTHER: You're not even ready? Quick-smart, we've got to get on the road, you know what traffic's like.

DRIZZLE BOY: Mum—

MOTHER: I swear, you say you're ready for the responsibility, but—

> *She helps him get into his space suit.*

You're gonna look smart in this.

DRIZZLE BOY: Mum, it's embarrassing—

MOTHER: No it isn't.

DRIZZLE BOY: I can do it myself—

MOTHER: I know you can, I just want to help.

She helps him into the last bit of his suit, tying shoelaces or some such.

DRIZZLE BOY: [*to the audience*] I once took the opportunity to tell someone who changed my life that everyone is made out of stardust. I wonder if the reason I am the way I am is because the bits of the universe that made me are held together in a different way. It's all about perspective.

MOTHER: Right, now I know you're nervous, but be scared and do it anyway.

DRIZZLE BOY: Mum, just stop for one second.

MOTHER: What? What is it?

They hold each other's gaze for a while. Pause.

DRIZZLE BOY: I love you, Mum.

She nods, and exits.

[*To the audience*] For as long as I can remember I've been trying to get to the stars. To escape. Not realising that for all the life out there, all the wonder, and joy … that there is just as much of it down here. I think part of the new dream is bringing all the majesty I see out in the universe down to Earth, to meet it halfway. Here.

The black hole dissolves into the planetarium.

STARLIGHT

Right Ascension 6 hours, 45 minutes, 9 seconds. Declination 16°, 42', 58".

Age nineteen.

Enter JULIET. DRIZZLE BOY *is in his space suit.*

JULIET: Hey.
DRIZZLE BOY: Hi.
JULIET: You're looking good.
DRIZZLE BOY: So are you.
JULIET: That's good.
DRIZZLE BOY: Good.
JULIET: We just said 'good' three times.
DRIZZLE BOY: That's not so good.
JULIET: Am I interrupting your shift?
DRIZZLE BOY: Nah. One sec.

He makes an announcement over the SPEAKER *system.*

Attention, ladies and gentlemen, the final showing of *Solar System Sailors* will begin in five minutes, thank you.
JULIET *and* DRIZZLE BOY: I should apologise.
DRIZZLE BOY: No, I should. Everything was too much for me all at once. No-one made any space for me except you. So I put everything on you. And that wasn't fair.

Pause.

JULIET: The planetarium, huh? It's kind of like you got the keys to the kingdom now. You always said you would go to the stars.
DRIZZLE BOY: And I get to see them every night. Your dad's technically part of the exhibit. Right ascension ten hours, twelve minutes, nineteen seconds. Declination—ninety degrees, twenty-five arcminutes, three arcseconds.
JULIET: You remembered.

DRIZZLE BOY: Of course.

JULIET: And is this what you want to do?

DRIZZLE BOY: Astronomy, I think. This place is a good start. What about you? What are you doing?

JULIET: Uni, semester two. Cramming for auditions for *Sound—*

Beat, she expects him to know.

—of Music.

They smile. Pause.

DRIZZLE BOY: You know, this wasn't a conversation we ever had. I didn't apologise to you.

JULIET: No?

DRIZZLE BOY: I never saw you again. I dropped out after first semester. You never returned my calls, and I figured no answer was an answer in itself. So I filled in the gaps. Imagining this seems good enough.

He begins the showing of Solar System Sailors.

Hello, everyone, are you all comfortable? Strapped in? Good. I'd like to take the opportunity now to tell you about the wonders of our universe. Today, we're going to take a look at comets. Comets fly past celestial bodies, but not always close enough to get pulled into their orbits.

He returns to his moment with JULIET.

So …

JULIET: You're letting me go.

DRIZZLE BOY: Slowly. Bits and pieces.

JULIET: Hey, what do you call a comet wrapped in bacon?

DRIZZLE BOY: I dunno, what?

JULIET: A meat-eor.

Pause.

DRIZZLE BOY: Bye, Julie.

JULIET: Bye, Drizzle Boy.

DRIZZLE BOY: Nobody calls me that any more.

She exits.

DRIZZLE BOY *talks to the audience one last time. He takes a small Earth in his hand.*

My life is a series of space–time coordinates. And at each of those coordinates there are moments—Floating within the universe— That have made me who I am. All I need to do is look up. I can see a mother desperately trying to get her son to eat anything other than frozen blueberries and she's crying because he won't. I see a young woman showing her signature dance move, the frustrated bumblebee, to a boy she likes or maybe even loves. I can vaguely make out a bright-eyed astronomer naming a new exoplanet after one of his father's favourite films. And lightyears away, I see a ten-year-old boy, standing on the roof as his parents yell at him to come down. He's staring at the stars, and dreaming of all the things that he might be. And I wish I could tell him there is nothing wrong with him. He's fine ... just the way he is. This will be my final transmission. I'm glad you're here. You and me. But I think from here on out, it's better if it's just me.

Enter BILL THE SPACE BEAR, *with the helmet of* DRIZZLE BOY's *suit.*

Oh. Hello. What's your name?

Bear noises. BILL *hands* DRIZZLE BOY *the helmet of his space suit.*

I thought as much. Well, I'm David. [*Aside*] It's very nice to meet you.

DAVID *puts on his helmet, takes* BILL *by the hand, and closes the face guard.*

THE END

www.ingramcontent.com/pod-product-compliance
Lightning Source LLC
Chambersburg PA
CBHW050020090426
42734CB00021B/3352